IN THE FOOTSTEPS
OF A SHADOW

In the Footsteps of a Shadow

North American Literary Responses to Fernando Pessoa

Edited by Charles Cutler,
Dan Mahoney & Gaby Gordon-Fox

MadHat Press
Cheshire, Massachusetts

MadHat Press
MadHat Incorporated
PO Box 422, Cheshire, MA 01225

Copyright ©2024 MadHatPress
Rights revert to individual poets

The Library of Congress has assigned
this edition a Control Number of
2024947228

ISBN 978-1-952335-88-4 (paperback)

Edited by Charles Cutler, Dan Mahoney & Gaby Gordon-Fox
Cover design by Marc Vincenz
Cover images by Sophia Santos

www.MadHat-Press.com

First Printing
Printed in the United States of America

I didn't want that "I" to be my "I." I wanted it to be an "I" that would take on the traffic of many personalities and personae and things.

—Nathaniel Mackey

He sees everything with their eyes.
He becomes not what they are but what they could be
If they weren't trapped in their characters.
For him, this new self of his is liberating because it's invented.

—Louise Glück

But the "I" isn't I anymore. It's someone else, the character who plays me, someone who's a better actor than I could ever be. I'm just the writer. Someone else is starring in my part. I remember him well enough to try to write about him. A case of the negative sublime.

—Charles Wright

… the urge to keep moving, to not look back, to shed one self in order to create another. That's really what I was getting at in the Bob Dylan biopic I'm Not There.

—Todd Haynes

We are reading the story of our lives,
as though we were in it,
as though we had written it.

—Mark Strand

Table of Contents

Acknowledgments — xvii
Letters from the Editors — xix
Introduction by Benjamin Kunkel
   A Cold in the Soul: Reading *The Book of Disquiet*
      in Apartment 62 — xxvii

Monteiro, George
   Hemispheric Pressures — xl

Accardi, Millicent Borges
   Inventing the Present — 3
Ansel, Talvikki
   After Pessoa — 5
Ashton, Sally
   I have no proof that Lisbon exists — 12
Bakken, Christopher
   Duet with Fernando Pessoa — 13
Baller-Shepard, Susan
   Doing the Math with Fernando — 15
   Herding Heteronyms — 16
Barnstone, Aliki
   Biographical Note on Eva Victoria Perera — 18
   Introducing Eva Victoria Perera — 21
Bassis, Aileen
   Watching A Stone — 28
Bernstein, Charles
   Autopsychographia — 29
   At Pessoa's Grave — 30
Biespiel, David
   Supremo Fernando — 31
Blaustein, Noah
   Flea/New House/Mutated Line of Pessoa's — 32
Bolling, Doug
   For Pessoa — 33
Bradley, John
   Footnote to a Line by Pessoa — 35
   How to Float — 37

Browne, Jenny
  Be Plural Like the Universe!   39
Buckley, Christopher
  I Too Am Not A Keeper of Sheep: Variations
    on a Theme by Pessoa   41
  Midnight Walk   45
Burton, Sue D.
  A Love Letter To Álvaro de Campos   47
Carpenter, William
  Clone   49
Carrillo, Albino
  Pessoa Crosses the Atlantic to Meet Some
    North Americans   51
Christiano, Roberto
  Sometimes It Is Necessary to be Someone Else   53
  The Terror of Wrestling the Masked Miguel Torquiero
    While Eating Baked Bread in Brazil   55
Christmas, Frank
  Caeiro Would Hold   58
Cigale, Alex
  The Spirit of Lindbergh   60
Cirino, Leonard
  Two from Ricardo Reis, The Sad Epicurean   62
  Contemplating The Keeper of the Sheep by the
    Unwitting Master, Alberto Caeiro   64
  Portrait of Fernando Pessoa   68
Collins, Billy
  The Day After Tomorrow   69
Czury, Craig
  from *Book Of Disquiet*: Deep Calls To Deep   71
Davis, Jon
  Commencement Address   73
  Notes To The Haitian Poems of Madeleine Du Plessix   76
  To Mr. Poe, From His Beautiful Annabel Lee   82
DeCarteret, Mark
  Slip   84
Dolin, Sharon
  Ode To Fernando Pessoa   85
Dryansky, Amy
  Untitled   89

Dunn, Stephen
    At the Restaurant   90
Dutterer, J. Paul
    The Gray Fables of Aesop S: July 29th   92
Ehrenberg, Erica
    Pessoa Is Willing   94
Emanuel, Lynn
    Walt, I Salute You!   95
Espinoza, Joshua Jennifer
    It Is Important to Be Something   97
Feinstein, Sandy
    Pen Names   98
Fillmore, Mary Dingee
    Love Stories   99
Finkelstein, Deborah
    Things   102
Gaspar, Frank
    I Am Not a Keeper of Sheep   104
    A Witness Gives His Version   106
Gastiger, Joseph
    Little Things That Get Lost   109
    In A Certain Light   110
    San Marino   111
Ginsberg, Allen
    Salutations to Fernando Pessoa   112
Glenn, Laura
    Faking It   115
Goldstein, David B.
    Burning Doll   117
Gorrick, Anne
    Jerry Freedman Thinks He's Fernando Pessoa   118
Gray, Robert
    A Selected Pose of Fernando Pessoa   120
Green, Timothy
    American Fractal   122
Haladay, Joan
    Trilha Pessoa   127
Hales, Daniel
    How To Converse with a Stranger   129

Hannaham, James
   Seeing and Thinking — 131
   Felt — 132
   The Person in Question — 133
   The Death of the Critic — 134
Hardy, Myronn
   Pessoa as Starling: New York City — 135
   Pessoa as Starling: Lisbon — 136
   Pessoa as Starling: Tunis — 137
   Pessoa as Starling: Johannesburg — 138
Harlan, Megan
   Ambient City — 139
   Painted Sky — 141
Hendricks, Jeanette
   Dizes-me: tu és alguma coisa — 142
   A espantosa realidade das coisas — 143
Hoagland, Tony
   The Question — 145
Holland, Walter
   After Pessoa — 147
Hoover, Paul
   Lisbon Story — 152
   I Am the Size of What I See — 154
Huenemann, Charlie
   Give Me Monotony! — 156
Irwin, Jason
   Rooms of My Life — 160
Jemc, Jac
   Expansion as Relief — 161
Kalamaras, George
   Fernando Pessoa, 1923 — 164
   Into the Moist — 166
   Fernando Pessoa Might Call My Body True — 167
Kartsonis, Ariana-Sophia
   Fernando Pessoa, I Salute You All! — 169
Ladin, Joy
   Fossilized Happiness — 173
Levine, Philip
   You Are You — 184

Lighthart, Annie
   In the Hour Favorable to Transformation   186
Lorenz, Johnny
   Oxcart   187
Mahoney, Daniel
   We Are Fernando   188
Maloney, Dennis
   Pessoa Café, Amsterdam   190
Margrave, Clint
   Pessoa Died a Virgin   192
Marvin, Cate
   Little Poem That Tries   193
Mastores, Constance Rowell
   Oxymoron   195
Medeiros, John T.
   faith   196
Merrill, Christopher
   Sagebrush   198
Monteiro, George
   Surface Noise   199
   Autobiography   200
   A Conceit   203
   Riding a Metaphor   204
Moss, Stanley
   An Exchange of Hats   205
Moure, Eirin
   Notes in Recollection   207
   What, me, guard sheep   210
   My sight's sharp as a sunflower   213
   What I'd give for my life to be my neighbour's old car   215
   Late yesterday in the Agora …   216
Radavich, David
   Split Infinitives   218
Rasmussen, Matthew
   Overnight   220
Ray, Jennifer Silke
   de Campos Mentis   221
Robinson, Elizabeth
   Having Words   222
   "a deeper breathing with other lungs"   224

Rogow, Zack
    Rant of a Drag Queen   226
Rudman, Mark
    Heteronym   228
Ryan, Kay
    Shipwreck   230
Sagan, Miriam
    After Pessoa   231
Samaras, Nicholas
    The Invented Man   232
Schneider, Ada Jill
    A Thought for Pessoa   234
Scrimgeour, J. D.
    The Sack   236
Seidel, Fredrick
    Homage To Pessoa   238
    Lisbon   239
Slate, Ron
    Shame   245
Springtail, Ken
    A Paean for Pessoa   247
Starkey, David
    Everything is Absurd   249
    The Windmill   251
Stephanie, S
    Oblique Question   252
Stein, D. L.
    Smoke   253
Stern, Gerald
    This Was a Wonderful Night   256
Tagliabue, John
    Weigh it in your hands, don't be noisy   258
    My being a poet isn't ambition, it's my way
        of being alone   259
Tolides, Tryfon
    November and Almost   260
Upton, Lee
    A Vast Journey   261
Vaz, Katherine
    My Prayer For Astonishment   262

Vincenz, Marc
    When Uncle Fernando Conjures Up a Dead-Bird
        Theory of Everything   274
Warren, Rosanna
    From the Notebooks of Anne Verveine   284
Washer, Naomi
    between me and the streets, and the home upstairs
        a fiction   289
Watson, Ellen Doré
    In Which I Address Fernando Pessoa   292
White, Jackie
    Voice Lessons: Fernando, To Fernando   293
Williams, John Sibley
    Only Half-Blind ... and Beautiful   295
    Language   297
    For Fernando Pessoa   299
Yakich, Mark
    The Teller Is the Only Survivor of the Fairytale Ending   301
    You Are Not a Statue   303
    Nocturne   305
    Yours and Some of Mine   306
Yates, Brenda
    Excerpt: A Review of *Absolutely, Positively 4th Street*   307
Yee, Amy
    Assignment #5: Pick a Word in Your Own Language
        and Describe What It Means   311

Contributors' Notes   313
Publication Credits   341

Acknowledgements

Charles

Because this anthology was years in the making, stemming from a time when I was working on it alone, my acknowledgments by themselves could fill a small book. First, I'm grateful for the encouragement I received from virtually all the writers who appear in this volume. Contributors and others often networked for me, providing leads to other potential participants. Among these activists on my behalf were George Kalamaras, Ariana-Sophia Kartsonis, Frank Gaspar, Katherine Vaz, Doug Bolling, Aliki Barnstone, Jon Davis, Talvikki Ansel, Ellen Doré Watson, Cate Marvin, George Monteiro, Susan Brown, Tryfon Tolides, and Alexis Levitin. Although not formerly part of the undertaking for the book, former Spanish and Portuguese Dept. colleagues and students at Smith College were there for me: Alice Clemente, Marguerite Itamar Harrison, Malcolm McNee, and Elizabeth Ginway.

I received enormous backing from poets Donald Hall, Philip Levine, Richard Wilbur, and W. S. Merwin who, one night, talked me through the plan for the book, later wrote me about it, and generously suggested I use "In the Footsteps of a Shadow" as a title.

Despite the early widespread enthusiasm for the anthology—also because of it—at one point, working alone, the project was clearly over my head and was running the risk of imploding. That's when my poet-editor-dear friend Dan Mahoney came to the rescue as co-editor, along with his associate Gaby Gordon-Fox. A fearless, multi-talented wunderkind, Dan was huge in bringing the anthology back to life and making it thrive. He sprinkled water on a stone turning it resplendent to the eye. Without Dan, there would have been no footsteps, just shadow.

Another key figure in the rescue squad was my compañera, Susan Olson, who, over the years, refused to let me sit down at the base of the mountain while watching the project disappear into the clouds.

And finally, thanks to my family for their good will, support, and, above all, for their endurance: They always managed to keep their eyes from glazing over on hearing the word "Pessoa" for the ten thousandth time.

Charles Cutler, Dan Mahoney & Gaby Gordon-Fox, eds.

Dan

Shout-out to all of the contributors who stuck with this project over its 20-year gestation. Big thanks to Colby College for offering two faculty development grants to support this project. Kristin Bock for her keen eyes and calming presence. Tomaž Šalamun for introductions. Dan Burt for being everywhere and nowhere at once. Lea Graham for showing the way. And, as always, a big thank you to the love at the center of my life: Harlan, Ruby & Judi.

Gaby

Thank you to everyone who, over the course of more than 20 years, was compelled to share their thoughts about this Portuguese poet whom they couldn't escape. Even after you've re-introduced me to him 1000 times, I'll never think that I know him. Perhaps I know 1000 iterations of him, or I don't know him at all. And I don't wish to. Full of greetings and farewells, this book for me is one of correspondences pieced together through long chains of sharing and held together with love and whatever keeps your fingers sticky.

Letters from the Editors

Pessoa & Charles

For me, the beginnings of *In the Footsteps of a Shadow* date back to the 1960s. At the time I was living in Lisbon where Pessoa, years after his death, was becoming a cultural icon. He was in the air, everywhere and nowhere at the same time, as was his way, always out of the corner of your eye. During his lifetime, acquaintances had often remarked that even off-the-page he was variable, capable of vanishing on the spot, now-you-see-me-now-you-don't. "Homem Fumo," smoke man. Given his phantom-like, flickering selves, it is perhaps strange that I should feel the rub and fall under his spell, but I did. The allure may have had something to do with identity restlessness in the '60s, a time when it seemed that many in my generation dreamed of being someone else, even multiplying themselves, often with "a little help from their friends." In this respect, Pessoa, with his ever-expanding company of selves, was a powerful magnet early on, however naive that attraction might seem in retrospect. Especially now, when reading *The Book of Disquiet*, Americans witness Pessoa unmasking the masks and erasing his game of mirrors in what appears to be a "suicidal" text.

The shared veneration for Whitman, though, was real. Pessoa's "Salutation to Walt Whitman" and the "Maritime Ode" had a profound effect on me, even more so during the time in Portugal than when reading those poems in the U.S. For one thing, they fed my nostalgia for home and because of their openness, optimism, and democratic spirit, they also acted as an antidote to the crushing repressiveness of the Salazar dictatorship at the time. In an oblique, underground, sort of way, I began thinking of Pessoa as an American poet. I remember dreaming that he was already in the U.S. when I returned from Portugal.

Pessoa's Whitman, his translations of Poe and his interest in other American writers, make a case by themselves for "dreaming America." In fact, though, they were part of a broader picture, that of his quasi-mystical take on Atlanticism and its enticing vision of cultural affinities between Western Europe and North America. In this regard, because of its ambiguity, Miguel Yeco's haunting painting (*A Mind by the Sea*) of Pessoa standing by the Atlantic suggests that he is on the North American side.

My early hunches about a compatibility between Pessoa and American writers were substantiated by Pessoa scholars, particularly George Monteiro and Irene Ramalho Santos: the former for his consideration of responses to Pessoa by Allen Ginsberg, Thomas Merton, and Lawrence Ferlinghetti and the latter for her remarkable insights into the interconnectedness and congeniality among Pessoa, Whitman, Hart Crane, Wallace Stephens, and Elliot.

Still, by far the strongest example of cultural solidarity between Pessoa and American culture, at least in my mind, is the echo chamber he shares with Bob Dylan. Dylan, the fellow Gemini, the shapeshifter, the many-sided one, always chameleonizing, always wrapped in myriad levels of impersonation. I like to think that Pessoa, wherever he might be, is giving me the nod. The affinity between the two, far from being conjecture on my part, is at the core of David Dalton's understanding of the singer-songwriter in his masterful *Who Is That Man? In Search of the Real Bob Dylan*. He begins his biography with a Pessoa roadmap to Dylan:

> Each of us is several, is many, is a profusion of selves. So the self who disdains his surroundings is not the same as the self who suffers or takes joy in them. In the vast colony of our being there are many species of people who think and feel in different ways.

Pessoa and Dylan, persona to persona, birds of a feather, twins of sorts, each other's other. Move over with your staid line "Je est un autre," Rimbaud, it's the Pessoa-Dylan band. "We should go on the road" and indeed they did, in yet another dream of mine. Antonio Tabucchi in his *Dreams of Dreams and The Last Three Days of Fernando Pessoa* suggests that the best way of knowing a favorite author is by dreaming their dreams. In "our" dream, Pessoa's and mine, he and

In the Footsteps of a Shadow

Dylan show up together at a packed gig in Northampton, MA, near where I live. Reciting, declaiming, singing Whitman poems, bringing the house down with a final vow: I'll let you be in my dream if I can be in your dream, I said that (we said that).

Pessoa & Dan

When the name "Fernando Pessoa" comes up in poetic circles it's best to stand back and let the volley of other names rain down around you: "Alberto Caeiro," "Álvaro de Campos," "Ricardo Reis" and on and on and on. Pessoa is one of those writers that inspires other writers to question who they think they are and what they think they're doing with who they think they are; not that writers don't already do this *ad nauseam*, but Pessoa gives them a precedent, a name to pin the vague feeling of imposterhood on. Part of the anxiety of being a contemporary poet is the fear of being found out as uninteresting, not very worldly ... an actual bore. Federico García Lorca had written several books and even more plays by the time he was assassinated in 1936; his name still circles the globe, a sort of talisman of what constitutes The Poet in the modern age. By the time contemporary poets come to grips with their terrible vocation (say, at age 20) they have visions of Lorca embedded in their dreams. By the time poets discover they are not Lorca (say, at age 25) there is this feeling of falling ... That is when Pessoa enters. He enters and he never leaves. I am reminded of Frank Gaspar's poem, "I Am Not a Keeper of Sheep":

> One must never let Pessoa across the threshold. I can say this
> with a sober mind for just a while longer. He sits
> so unassumingly at the table and you give him a small drink,
> and he begins to speak to you, and then you realize your day is
>   ruined,
> your plans will come to nothing, you will end by trying
> every subterfuge you know to get him to leave, but he will wait
> and wait.

I first encountered Pessoa in the anthology *Another Republic*, edited by Charles Simic and Mark Strand, but Pessoa did not make a huge impact on me until I was in graduate school taking a writing workshop with Tomaž Šalamun who had us young writers reading *The Book of Disquiet*. I began reading *Disquiet* during a particularly bad winter in western Massachusetts, one that kept me inside smoking more, drinking more ... hibernating. Books were my only companions those days. By that time, I understood I was no Lorca and was unsure of what I actually was. I sat at the window looking for something I could not name. Leonard Cirino, in "Portrait of Fernando Pessoa," nails this feeling: "Fernando would sit by the window / all day, waiting for something to happen / while he smoked without peace, in a silence he hoped would remove him from the world." Those days. I was so goddamn lonely and uncertain and lost, I wanted to disappear.

Armed with *Disquiet*—and having failed to meet the grand stature of The Poet—I became absence, a wolf abandoning all four feet in the trap. I began writing album reviews for bands and albums that didn't exist. I wrote hundreds of these, each from a different point of view. I considered the reviews coming from the hands of employees working in an immense record store, each one steeped in the vocabulary of their discrete microgenre, their singular macrosound. I woke up at 4 a.m. each morning and tried to transcribe not only what these people said but how they said it. In order to listen I became an emptiness in search of other voices, like the speaker in one of Elizabeth Robinson's poems, "I didn't want / the womb which is a blank screen; I wanted / this endlessness, someone else's air pinned to / my own breath." Emptiness became my poetic salvation.

Lonely children create myriads of playmates out of thin air until they don't, until their parents or teachers or friends let them know there is only value in the single, the *E pluribus unum*, the unified self. And then a deeper loneliness grows inside them. Pessoa never stopped creating characters to interact with. Having very little interest in the stock writers—especially contemporary writers—put into "finding your own voice," Pessoa sent missive after missive, heteronym after heteronym to fill the world with voices and, in doing so, became the 20th-century embodiment of Walt Whitman's "I contain multitudes." Whitman, however, filtered his multitudes into a grand poetic vision in version after version of *Leaves of Grass*. His face became the face of the multitudes he wrote about, and he carefully crafted a look that has become more famous, more recognizable, than any single poem he wrote. Pessoa, on the other hand, just disappears: *E unum pluribus*.

Not to say that reading Whitman's work did not have a profound impact on Pessoa. It did. One of Pessoa's heteronyms, Álvaro de Campos, is a Whitmanian through and through. The ode, "Salutation to Walt Whitman," written in 1915 by de Campos, makes Pessoa's affinity for Whitman clear, "At any given moment, reading your poems, I can't tell if I'm reading or living them." Lynn Emanuel and Allen Ginsberg riff on the expansive voice in de Campos' ode with greetings of their own. Emanuel, in "Walt, I Salute You!" announces: "Here we are. In Love! In a Poem! / Slouching toward rebirth in our hats and curls! / Walt, I'm just a woman, chaperoned, actual, vague and hysterical!" while Ginsberg, in "Salutations to Fernando Pessoa" uses a slightly different tack, "Everytime I read Pessoa I think / I'm better than he is I do the same thing / more extravagantly—he's only from Portugal, / I'm American greatest Country in the world ..."

With multitudes of avatars interacting with each other in the digital universe, our age has finally caught up with Pessoa. We open our computers and from a lonely room we become a throng: buying, selling, creating, augmenting, insulting, roving at will, being other than we are. There is great creative freedom in heteronymity. The hip hop world, while valorizing "keeping it real," knows this fact more intimately than other artistic movements; rappers regularly create a multitude of voices to help them access shards of truth, from Eminem's Slim Shady, Nicki Minaj's Roman Zolanski, Megan Thee Stallion's Tina Snow, and Gunna's Wunna, to Kool Keith's run of more than 58 heteronyms including Dr. Octagon, Dr. Doom, Black Elvis, and Crazy Lou. But how can rappers (and poets, for that matter) be real and fake at once? Charles Bernstein's version of Pessoa's "Autopsychographia" shows us the way:

Poets are fakers / Whose faking is so real
They even fake the pain / They truly feel

To paraphrase Kevin Young, real pain masked by fake pain, that's the dance, the place where rap—and poetry—is born.

When my book of music reviews came out, my name was on it, but I really didn't know who had composed those reviews. What I remember most about the writing was sitting at 4 in the morning, a hole in the air around me, trying to listen. In the words of Christopher Merrill, "… the voices running through my lines seem to come from somewhere else, in the manner of his heteronyms. Pessoa taught me how to listen."

I met Charles Cutler around this time. He was older than me, an east coaster, a Celtics/Red Sox fan, carried around a fly rod, and a resonator guitar. I did not know what to make of him, but I fell in love with his lust for life, music, and poetry. He was besotted with Pessoa and was collecting work for an upcoming anthology. I told him to wait a second … told him I had something … that was more than 20 years ago.

Pessoa & Dan & Charles

So here we are years later, in a time when Pessoa seems a perfect antidote to the celebration of fame, image, success, stupidity, convenience, noise, and other forms of "myopia" (Pessoa's term). A time when many of us are anxious to explore and reconcile alternative versions of ourselves, of being human, perhaps even contemplating invisibility in its myriad guises (Akiko Busch). The urgency in this regard has accounted, at least in part, for the intense and widespread interest in our anthology as well as for the desire to be part of it.

Thus, we have whittled a bunch of strong work into what you see in this book, a whole new contingent for Pessoa's extended "family." In his life Pessoa published not one but two books in English, the language he had always regarded as a surer way to greatness than Portuguese. Although while alive he never achieved that greatness in the English-speaking world, there are many now who have pursued the goal on his behalf: translators Edwin Honig, Susan Brown, Richard Zenith, Chris Daniels, Margaret Jull Costa, and others; Pessoa scholars, particularly those considering the American connection such as George Monteiro and Irene Ramalho Santos; and of course, Richard Zenith's recent mammoth Pessoa biography. One thing is for sure: *In the Footsteps of a Shadow* attests to the growing presence of Pessoa in the American cultural space beyond university circles. It is also clear that Pessoa's continuum of identities is a breath of fresh air for American writers, especially poets. For them, he offers an escape from what Chris Daniels refers to as the "monopoly of the self," authorial ownership, and "expectations of emotional truth." Our hope is that the anthology will help to further expand that presence in the coming years, bringing Pessoa out of his country of dream into what he once called the American universe of flesh and bone.

Introduction

A Cold in the Soul: Reading The Book of Disquiet *in Apartment 62*

I don't know why I picked up Fernando Pessoa's *The Book of Disquiet*. But it would have required some monster of perfect well-being not to be attracted by the title alone, not to suspect that such a book might contain examples of his own admissions and evasions. The book can't have been recommended to me, since no one I know had read it, which I always liked: it permitted me as I read Pessoa not only the lightly sinister pleasure of a minor vice, but that sensation of guilty singularity that attaches itself to any good vice as well. See, *The Book of Disquiet* (sitting by my bedside over almost a year as hundreds of glasses of water were drained and filled) really did function, more than anything else I've ever read, as a vice, or a small suffusing sin, or a chronic low-level illness—"like having a cold in the soul," to borrow from Pessoa.

Anyone thus congested will want to stay at home—and if he goes out will catch a strange timbre in the voice he overhears as his own and feel a once removed slipping in and out of his gestures even as he makes them. Yet I (who am one of those young and lucky, aspiring people in New York) often went out at night after having looked into *The Book of Disquiet* earlier on, and when I did, this breviary of loneliness and melancholy and failure seemed to introduce a flutter of hesitation into my actions, compromising my ready smile and tinting with hypocrisy all my usual desires. And what are those? The standard issue. It would be nice to have success, love, and money in the right degree. I have this image of a table surrounded by laughing friends, maybe including—I can't quite see this—my future wife. It seems we all have done well for ourselves, and perhaps I have done just a little better than the rest.

So at times I have imagined that this favorite book of mine, *The Book of Disquiet*, has done more damage to my professional and social and romantico-sexual and general all-purpose human career than any other has. Here in the famously striving city I'd been infected by a book whose credo, if it has one, is that "Inaction is our consolation for everything, not acting our one great provider." Pessoa lived alone (like me!). He never married (so far, so good), and is only known to have kissed a woman once (the parallel collapses). He rarely left the city of Lisbon, even for the weekend, (this part works, *mutatis mutandis*) and throughout his writing he denigrates travel as a poor substitute for his fantasies of the same (more and more I agree with him there). It seems the least tribute his loyal reader can pay him is to have misgivings about leaving the apartment.

But officially *The Book of Disquiet* belongs not to Fernando Pessoa, who while contriving to make his real existence as light a phenomenon as possible nevertheless had to eat and breathe (and drink and chain-smoke). Pessoa wanted the book credited to Bernardo Soares, a pretended acquaintance and actual pseudonym, who naturally didn't exist at all. If reading Soares's book made me feel fractionally different from myself, then how much more strongly must Pessoa have felt this as he set down Soares's words. And maybe this mild and eerie sensation—as if when you looked into a mirror your bifocal vision failed you, so that there were two figures there, mostly overlapping but both transparent—has been transmitted from author to reader.

Pessoa was as devoted to incompleteness as to self-estrangement, and most of the prose he wrote was fragments. In one fragment, he says that Bernardo Soares was an assistant bookkeeper for a fabric warehouse, someone Pessoa used to run into when "economic necessity" forced him to frequent one of the cheap Lisbon "restaurants or eating places, which have the stolid, homely look of those restaurants you see in towns that lack even a train station." Pessoa credited his various texts to at least seventy-two different people, and he called these invented figures, some equipped with complex biographies, his "heteronyms." Within the huge clan of heteronyms, Soares is the only "semi-heteronym." And in what way was Soares merely somewhat other? He was—and here's the dry extravagance of Pessoa's humor—"myself minus reason and affectivity."

In the Footsteps of a Shadow

I wonder if Pessoa somewhere recorded the date of his first meeting Soares. It wouldn't have been uncharacteristic. Ricardo Reis, who, among Pessoa's heteronyms, is one of the most prolific, reports that he never wrote a line before meeting another of the three, Alberto Caeiro, one day at the age of twenty-five. I think of this decisive encounter of imaginary people alongside my own discovery, because it is Pessoa's sense, and mine, that real people too are mostly imaginary—in that they imagine far more life than they lead.

*

So I walked out of Labyrinth Books with a paperback in hand. Maybe this was late in the afternoon and the air was suitably moist. A mizzling rain; the light nacreous, diffuse, and failing; today resigning itself to becoming yesterday ... That, at any rate, is the tone of *The Book of Disquiet*, a book at once nervous and damp, where passage after passage takes note of the rain off the ocean, and the light seems always to be "this indefinite lucid blue pallor of the aquatic evening."

Yet the event just as easily might have occurred on a poundingly hot day, a Friday, say, and after starting to read on the subway— "Today, during one of those periods of daydreaming which, though devoid of purpose, still constitute the greater part of the spiritual substance of my life..."—I may have emerged downtown onto streets taken up by a bright jostling carnival of competitive glamour, and there I may have had a sort of everyday vision. (This was when the city knew itself as the headquarters of a boom rather than as the prey of terrorists.) I would see some put-together person, relaxed but intent, who seemed to know just where he was going. The impression was of his doing what he was meant to and being not the least bit divided against himself: He has served his ambition as the obvious and only good and is in the middle of a long success. This is a New York type, harder to describe but as much a part of the scene as the scissory women and round-shouldered delivery men, the beggars, the police, the tourists; and if that figure is what I saw in one or another of his versions, then I must also have been assailed by a pitifully simple and common fantasy, which is that I too will get to be a successful and admired person in this apparent capital of the world.

Charles Cutler, Dan Mahoney & Gaby Gordon-Fox, eds.

In any case, I've forgotten the date. It's disheartening not to be able to mark an important anniversary. For me *The Book*'s counsel of renunciation—"Whatever we renounce, we preserve intact"—leaked over a year into the close atmosphere of New York City, with its roast and exhaust of immodest aspiration. The city that never sleeps ... and reading Pessoa, who wanted to write "an apotheosis of sleep," made me feel like an emotional dissident here, someone eager to do without exactly what he wanted most. Which is why if I eventually fail in what I've come here to do, a portion of blame should probably be laid at the apartment door, to be found on Lisbon's Rua dos Douradores, of the imaginary assistant bookkeeper Bernardo Soares who with his "inert soul of a born abdicator" anticipated, when dreaming of literary glory, the nostalgia he might someday suffer "for this uncertain life in which I scarcely write at all and publish nothing."

It's been a while now since I finished *The Book of Disquiet*. A favorite book from the start, I read it more slowly than if it was a chore. For one thing, the book consists of aphorisms, some as short as a single line, others as long as three pages, and to read too many at once would have muddled the arguments of them all. Not that *The Book* isn't of a piece. In its determined melancholy, its gentle audacity, and in its insistence on renunciation, frustration, and solitude as the nectars of life, it is almost scarily whole.

Improbably, too, when you consider that no one knows how to put the individual parts together. Pessoa, born in 1888, announced *The Book of Disquiet* as forthcoming in 1914, but this was not to be. The work was published posthumously, as all true odes to frustration should be. *Livro do Desassossego*, "the saddest book in Portugal," Pessoa called it, didn't appear in his city of Lisbon until 1982, forty-seven years after his death from cirrhosis of the liver at the age of forty-seven. The entries of this "factless autobiography"— from which it's impossible to learn of any meals taken, trips set out on, jobs completed, friends entertained, or women courted—were written between 1912 and 1935, the year of Pessoa's death, and are, according to the translator of my edition, "frequently undated and undateable." At least 27,543 documents—more than two for each day of Pessoa's solitary and graphomaniacal adult life (so much for scarcely writing at all)—are to be found in the Pessoa archives in Lisbon, and while he clearly indicated many passages as belonging to the Livro, and as being written by Soares, just as many are included on the basis of scholarly conjecture.

This editorial chaos almost seems a part of Pessoa's design. *The Book of Disquiet* is a diary, but of a self that is several and precarious, and always more potential than actual. Its floating boundaries expand and contract, lazily animated by "the horror of making our soul a fact." As Pessoa/Soares writes, "I'm always astonished whenever I finish anything. Astonished and depressed. My desire for perfection should prevent me from ever finishing anything; it should prevent me even from starting." Presumably it was this desire that prevented Pessoa from publishing more than one book in Portuguese during his life. That was a book of poetry, a nationalistic collection called *Mensagem* (*Message*), and for many years Pessoa was known only as a poet, Portugal's greatest since the equally nationalistic Camões. He and his three main heteronyms are indeed very good poets, but it seems that it was as Soares and in the prose of *The Book of Disquiet*, where he wrote of the "desire to die another person beneath unknown flags," that he found himself more truly.

My edition of *The Book*—among the infinite possibilities, at least three exist in English—is translated, beautifully, by Margaret Jull Costa. It follows a thematic selection by Pessoa scholar Maria José de Lancastre, who has clustered the passages around such themes as dreams, weariness, ambition, affections, landscapes, rain. Reading a page or two a day, I would find myself curiously preoccupied along certain lines for a week or more—weird: in the sunlight I'd been thinking constantly of rain—and then the topic would change and, like a spell of weather, move on. I suppose this is just as well if Pessoa is right and

> No problem is soluble. None of us unties the Gordian knot; we either give up or cut it. We brusquely resolve with our feelings problems of the intellect and do so because we are tired of thinking, because we are too timid to draw conclusions, because of an absurd need for support, or because of our gregarious impulse to rejoin the others and rejoin life.

*

Yet slow immersion in *The Book* gave me some trouble in setting it aside and rejoining, without compunction, my gregarious colleagues in youth and ambition and—in one instance—love. It wasn't only the heavy emphasis laid on renunciation, a rare pleasure at a time when nothing else around you seems to honor or recognize such a thing. *The Book* also reflects and encourages an elaborate solitude. The trouble with such a solitude is that the more elaborate it becomes, the more difficult it is to haul into the light of an ordinary conversation. Even a uniquely subtle conversation will violate its constitutive contradictions.

When I thought of love, I would imagine enjoying a type of communion with another honest, articulate being. But throughout the Pessoa phase, the Pessoa year, I was becoming less and less forthright: hard to confess to your girlfriend your growing delight in solitude. And in talking about anything that mattered, I was always aware of that remainder of the insoluble problem which the words left behind, as if I were constantly failing at a simple problem of division. Now I missed being single, with its license to be shapeless and confused. The old promise—finally being known—had become a menace to the delicate incoherencies I was nurturing. Love seemed to want to enforce my identity as someone I had never, not liking to choose, wholeheartedly chosen to be.

"You don't seem all the way in this," she said, my girlfriend.

If there were ever someone to be in something with, it would have been her, so I thought, for reasons like the reasons anyone has in these cases. Besides, it pleased me when I could make this good and attractive person happy. So I said, "I am in this, all the way." Meanwhile it was clear to me that nice guys are in fact dangerous people, and I remembered *The Book of Disquiet*: "I have a very simple morality: not to do evil or good to anyone."

*

Kafka is always quoted as saying that a great book should function like "an axe to break up the frozen sea within us." The image calls to mind a weekend spent indoors with a book, a short fatal siege. But it may be that a book is most affecting when read in dribs and drabs over many months. Troubling and even repugnant at the outset, it becomes familiar, and by dint of prolonged exposure to the poison we become immune to it. The term is mithridatism, and the best illustration is Hawthorne's Beatrice Rappaccini, a lovely virgin to whom the world outside her artificial paradise, all concocted of poison, becomes a fatal toxin.

Susan Sontag (the point of quoting all these people is to suggest a certain book-bound existence) once wrote that writers are either husbands or lovers. There are also confirmed bachelors. And Pessoa, who almost certainly died a virgin, is the great bachelor of modernism—entirely singular, solitary, and aloof. In photographs the appearance is always the same, his face like a disguise picked up at a novelty shop: the big nose attached to the thick black glasses, the thin unsmiling lips almost concealed by a little moustache. The fedora, bowtie, and raincoat are likewise invariable, and the whole effect is of neutrality-of-being carried almost to the point of non-existence. Photographs seek to prove that we exist, but Pessoa appears to be trying to tamper with the evidence—an impression that wouldn't be worth much, except that his writing ratifies it so completely.

The system of the heteronyms allowed him to disown his words even as he wrote them. The heteronyms formed a small society of alter egos, "a whole world of friends inside me," and they were united above all by their conviction that the soul has no product. That is, any deed immediately estranges itself from its doer, and travesties the intention behind it. It becomes alien. "Every gesture, however simple, represents a violation of a spiritual secret," Pessoa writes. "To act is to exile oneself." The same goes for emotions, those interior gestures: one day, "Nothing will remain of the person who put on feelings and gloves"—just as if those were the same.

Certain philosophers passed much of the twentieth century in an effort to exorcise the ghost of Descartes—to rid us of the notion that every self is split between subject and object, one who is versus one who thinks, a watcher versus a doer. But Pessoa represents a kind of kudzu Cartesianism: a crazy interior multiplication of egos, each thought or feeling producing a separate spectator self, a subject then made into the object of a brand new subject, and so on indefinitely. From *The Book of Disquiet*:

> I created various personalities within myself. I create them constantly. Every dream, as soon as it is dreamed, is immediately embodied by another person who dreams it instead of me.
>
> In order to create, I destroyed myself; I have externalized so much of my inner life that even inside I now exist only externally.

*

The more I've learned about Pessoa, the better I seem to understand how one of Gustave Doré's illustrations for *The Divine Comedy* frightened him all his life: Canto 13, the Forest of the Suicides. There a multitude of people dead by their own hands turn ineluctably into objects, namely trees. Self-destroyed, they exist only outside themselves, and this externalization is the internal experience they have to go on suffering.

But if that is the infernal image of Pessoa's work, *The Book of Disquiet* most often seduced me as a perversely cheerful apologia for withdrawal from everything, for "the sweetness of having neither family nor companions, the gentle pleasure akin to that of exile, in which we feel the pride of distance shade into a hesitant voluptuousness." Behold the paradise of Bernardo Soares: "A cup of coffee, a cigarette, the penetrating aroma of its smoke, myself sitting in a shadowy room with my eyes half-closed."

Elsewhere he is more elaborate: "To live a dispassionate, cultured life beneath the dewfall of ideas, reading, dreaming and thinking about writing, a life slow enough to be always on the edge of tedium, but considered enough not to slip into it. To live a life removed from emotions and thoughts, enjoying only the thought of emotions and the emotion of thoughts. To stagnate, golden, in the sun like a dark lake surrounded by flowers." The best guess is that the bending flowers themselves are narcissi.

*

And it's easy and correct enough to say that Pessoa and his work are simply narcissistic. He and the heteronyms seem intent on nothing so much as their arrested development; they are lifelong adolescents, addicts of potential. The less one acts, the more potential is conserved, or so you can believe. Pessoa and Soares et al. are not, therefore, the best group to fall in with in your twenties. The big task of people my age, those who haven't yet found a partner or exactly settled on a profession, must be to enter the really existing world without getting broken in the process, to distinguish realism from selling-out and also ideals from excuses. Pessoa's work, on the other hand, is testimony to the melancholy pleasure of shirking this task permanently and devotedly. Like a temp, Soares has taken his job as an assistant bookkeeper reluctantly, because he must: "Anyone reading the earlier part of this book will doubtless have formed the opinion that I'm a dreamer. If so, they're wrong. I don't have enough money to be a dreamer." But this only means that he lacks enough to dream full-time. Getting called a good-for-nothing would not affront him. He enjoys quoting the French philosopher Gabriel Tarde: "Life is a search for the impossible via the useless."

Work and love are alleged to be the keys to happiness, but Soares and Pessoa, who have each other, demur. Pessoa is never more audacious, characteristic, or sinister than when he says such things as: "Woman is a rich source of dreams. Never touch her." Friendship doesn't fare much better in his account: "The only possible reason for asking other people's advice is to know, when we subsequently do exactly the contrary of what they told us to do, that we really are ourselves, acting in complete disaccord with all that is other."

All throughout the year of my reading *The Book of Disquiet* I was also finishing up grad school; making a first go of a freelance career; eating and dressing a little better than before, and a little beyond my means; hanging out with the friends who have, like me, ended up in the huge funnel of New York; and alternately suffering and enjoying an on-again, off-again love affair, or *affaire maudite*, with that girlfriend whom I loved and often avoided. I was also working on a novel—the completion of which seemed to recede further away the more I wrote. I'm referring to "the horror of making our soul a fact." Yet it doesn't seem impossible or even all that unlikely that I will more or less get what I want and what I'd come here for, in this city that more than any other is consecrated to such desires. No doubt I would have hesitated in the face of a threatened fulfillment no matter what book I'd left by my bedside for months, but it remains hard to imagine one that would have more exacerbated my hesitations, or better improved upon them, as the case may be, than *The Book of Disquiet*. "I like to read the way a chorus girl does," E. M. Cioran writes, "identifying myself with the author and the book." So it is for me too. In many ways Pessoa and I couldn't be more different. My politics are to the left, I'm reasonably abstemious, I travel when I can, I have more than enough friends, and to my barbaric ear, Portuguese—Pessoa's "clear, majestic language"—sounds like Spanish as spoken by Eastern Europeans. Yet *The Book of Disquiet*, the work of a royalist loner and virgin dead sixty-seven years ago from too much drink, has often seemed as intimate a book as if the words were mine. At times it was as if someone had drawn up my confession, to which I need only supply the crime.

I seemed to savor my life by my reluctance to live it. The romance I was in, as I finished *The Book of Disquiet*, was presumed to be ending again, and again not actually acting like it was. In my politics too there were issues of "commitment." The power of my left-wing analysis seemed constantly to increase while—despite the rallies attended, the petitions signed—the power of the left itself steadily diminished. And the great novel I was writing I suspended or abandoned in order to work on something shorter and less important to me. Even in small things—what to do next week with a friend—I was hesitant and uncertain. Decisiveness seemed to shear the edges off time, permitting the days to lapse by too quickly, and I didn't know—I still don't—any better way of slowing things down than to enter a pleasant little agony of abulia. *The Book of Disquiet*, involved in all this, had become my book of hours.

It's not that its philosophical contents couldn't be found elsewhere. I could have re-read Emerson on self-reliance. I could have adopted the opinion Proust labored to adopt, over thousands of pages, on the emptiness of friendship and love. I could have remarked, with Samuel Beckett in his study of Proust, on "the nullity of what we are pleased to call attainment." Even Joseph Conrad, temperamentally so different from those others, wrote in *Nostromo* that "Action is consolatory. It is the enemy of thought and the friend of flattering illusion."

But I think my susceptibility to Pessoa's "cold in the soul" had to do with his own susceptibility. Where the others make arguments, he confesses himself in fragments. The transvaluation of values he proposes—all the customary grails turned upside down—is more persuasive to me than Nietzsche's much more strenuous operation, not only because Pessoa will have nothing to do with the despicable will-to-power, but because he suffers his truths at least as much as he advances them. After all, he is giving things up not because he doesn't want them, but because he does. The image of the Gordian knot isn't an idle one:

> The further we advance in life, the more we become convinced of two contradictory truths. The first is that, confronted by the reality of life, all the fictions of literature and art pale into insignificance… They are just dreams from which one awakens, not memories or nostalgic longings with which we might later live a second life.
>
> The second is this: every noble soul wishes to live life to the full, to experience everything and every feeling, to know every corner of the earth and, given that this is impossible, life can only be lived to the full subjectively, only lived in its entirety once renounced.
>
> These two truths are mutually irreducible.…
>
> Nothing satisfies me, nothing consoles me, everything—whether or not it has ever existed—satiates me. I neither want my soul nor wish to renounce it. I desire what I do not desire and renounce what I do not have. I can be neither nothing nor everything: I'm just the bridge between what I do not have and what I do not want.

*

This bridge—Pessoa is often writing about bridges—is also between the self and the world. Pessoa's intuition was that the two could not both be real at once. Meanwhile there was the bridge, nothing solid on either side.

These days it often seems to me high time that I try to take a single shape in the world, that I make a sincere effort to live the best of my possible lives. At such times my way of reading *The Book of Disquiet* appears in retrospect as a bad habit and a symbol of undisclosed troubles. What did this book do for me but aggravate my indecision and help perfect my bad conscience? The advice anyone would give is to get it together and be serious, and although I can quote chapter and verse against this counsel—"The world belongs to the unfeeling. The essential condition for being a practical man is the absence of any sensitivity"—I feel guilty not taking it.

And there are other arguments to be made against Pessoa-ism, or Soares-itis, or whatever it is. For one thing, Pessoa rarely specifies the contents of his dreams, and while this strange emptiness invites the reader to take the book as his own, it doesn't only do that. It also breeds the suspicion that Pessoa is more capable of relishing his dreams than of having them. For how long can he keep up their production without believing in or really desiring their realization?

Yet just as often as I am tempted to give in to misgivings and guilt, I feel something else—I feel that I'm right to clutch the thought of *The Book* to me, and to prefer, to any satisfaction I might obtain, the excitement and dread of being solitary and unrealized. This is especially so when I'm back in my apartment, alone with my books. Then I wonder again if it's true that "Freedom is the possibility of isolation." Meanwhile, "Life, obvious and unanimous, flows past outside me in the footsteps of the passers-by." All that is quoting Pessoa, with whom I may have identified too strongly, as a patient becomes a part of his disease, or disquiet. Yet the ideal reader is an invalid. He lies in bed and imagines the life he might lead once recovered. If the illness is prolonged, what was a chance occurrence, an event separate from him, alters his character somewhat and becomes a part of it. Of course, I'm not sick at all, and in reading *The Book of Disquiet* I took all the pleasure that is the mark of good health. Nevertheless, even now that I haven't taken the book down from its shelf in my bedroom for several months, sometimes when I am walking through New York, with its hurry and din and its large portion of purposeful and enviable people (I have sometimes even heard that I am one of them), I look around and think, thinking of *The Book of Disquiet*, "I'll never set foot in this world." Whether this sentence, uttered silently in a voice not quite my own, amounts to a boast, a bizarre lie, or a statement of sad fact is one of many things I don't know and, if the example of Pessoa is any guide, may contrive never to learn.

—Benjamin Kunkel

George Monteiro

Hemispheric Pressures

He could not have written Frost's "Road Not Taken." One of his heteronyms could have, but their progenitor could not have, since with them, he walked down all the roads he cared to walk. It's odd that the American wrote his poem in the same year that, in Lisbon, the poet's inexistent coterie first made the primal scene in his bedroom.

In the Footsteps of a Shadow

Millicent Borges Accardi

Inventing the Present

> *Far away, far away, far away from here ... There's no running after joy, or away from fear, Far away from here.*
> —Pessoa

This time I stick through
the aches pulling at me

like the flu left alone.
To co-habitate, to move

back, these chains tightening.
Of coupling, the welcome

home into a comfortable time,
to a round object. The state

of two halves restored,
of being apple, then carved.

The feeling of wholeness
lost and returned.

The secure luxury of
being on the tree, fearless.

Back into ripe growth
and then magically fused

Charles Cutler, Dan Mahoney & Gaby Gordon-Fox, eds.

with another. That happens.
The lull, coming home to a warm

body, the checking in. The awful
noise that ends where one

begins and is later part of two,
the noise you hate but cannot vocalize.

Each time stopping to sing, apologizing
to the earth for the rest of your life.

Talvikki Ansel

After Pessoa

Today I was quiet, and sat in a corner
where I never had before. Through the closet's
glass door—the hall with the same light
that smoothed trunks of high-bush blueberries
the spring I was nineteen. Some weeks
on the island I'd never see another person,
hear an outboard motor. Every morning
I reached a mirror on a bamboo pole
into trees, over the herons' eggs that floated
in the circular reflection above my head,
opaque and hard. Floating a slide now
in the lamplight I see how I held the camera
 to one side over the sink, in a blue shirt
I've seen in pictures of my mother.

*

I'm reading *The Book of Disquietude*
and now while I stand by the window it's
Pessoa I keep talking to as I think
how much I like looking—at the grit-rooved
houses, my yellow chair. He likes
the pattern in the blue linoleum,
but he's not sure where to put his hat.
I call "hi, come in," from the top
of the landing. Tap, tap of shoe nails
on stair treads.

Charles Cutler, Dan Mahoney & Gaby Gordon-Fox, eds.

Pessoa, why
did you write, "for a long time now I haven't
existed," and, "I'm like a traveler
who suddenly finds himself in a strange town?"

*

He thinks it's strange
I write to him since he's dead,
he says—
why question *The Book
of Disquietude* in
infinitesimal detail (which
by the way, I wrote
in an alcoholic haze and can't
imagine reading now
in its entirety).

And—
I was never much
for bird eggs, except
pickled with beer,
you're confused, so
confused you write to me,
repeat the lines I've written.

*

"… But the city is unknown to me, and streets new and the sickness without a cure."

"There's a thin sheet of glass between me and life." (*The Book
of Disquietude* #76)

The gull pulls a moon shell into her nest
because it is the size of an egg—this
her cure for longing, a way to fill
a space, a shape, hollow in the grass
where a third egg could be, *saudade*. Pessoa, "love
is what you need," was what
I was going to write. But what
do I know? Nights when the kitchen was too cold
and dark to read, I listened to the weather radio,
"1.45 megahertz from Blue *Hill*
Massachusetts," knots, waves. In bed I wore
all my clothes, a mound of blankets, comforters,
yet still felt myself hovering, nowhere,
unweighted, emphasis on *hill*.

*

"I have a tender spot—tender to the point of tears—for my
ledgers in which I keep other people's accounts, for the old
inkstand I use..." (#7)

For her, as she kneels in the sun by the Briggs
& Stratton motor, pulls the starter cord
to pump the day's water. And you writing
on a white sandwich wrapper, turning a glass
slowly, at the table of a Lisbon café.
For how she imagined a friend
appearing on the lawn: a walk, talk—words,

gestures, lashes, eyes. (If she spoke now
what would she say?) She reads and re-reads
her mail—the familiar scrawl
sits beside her on the back step, whispers,
whispers fervently in her ear. She feels
visited, how after a dream you might
treat a person differently in morning.

*

"In Lisbon, my sad town,
the dead letter office
like a cage of unread birds
fluttering. So many letters
I thought I'd write
imagined reading …
I gestured on my walks,
my quick retorts!
It was almost as if
I had a friend to write
to me. I invented
Caeiro my master.
We read each other's
poems, I shook his hand.
We laughed, almost
knocked heads above
the café table, sparrows
rose and settled. He had
a monocle like me—single
glass oval glinting …"

In the Footsteps of a Shadow

*

Below the plane, white crustaceans
on a whale's head, minute spray of gannets
diving, flat gray blanket of distance.
Stone walls on the island—rows of beads.
I couldn't see myself walking, upright, alive,
holding an egg to my face to test
its warmth. The Beechcraft in the air, whales
in the water. No calls today, no mail.
Somewhere, a girl pretends she is a river,
imagines rain falling into her. I would tell her
these things matter to her, though
she may or may not see them.

*

You are the words when all the lights go out
and hunch-backed Sergio
leaves off the invoices and goes home.
You put the sheep to lambing behind a stone wall,
when there's still snow on the ground, starry-fleeced,
and the daffodils are silly with yellow.
You make the shepherd slit the dead lamb's
belly, wrap its skin around the orphan's back.
He carries the lamb, swathed in another's smell,
to find a sheep … On the street a laughing
couple passes, you think, "too beautiful
for me"—you think you feel the longing
before bird song, absurd. Consolation—a wheel
of cheese, wine, a white sandwich wrapper.

Charles Cutler, Dan Mahoney & Gaby Gordon-Fox, eds.

*

"Sometimes I think how beautiful it would be if I could
join my dreams together and make them a continuous life,
a life consisting of entire days of companions and created
people...." (*The Book of Disquietude* #116)

Pessoa, the light on Douradores Street
still reddens the tiles, gilds roofs. Why
did you lie in your book, write that your mother
died when you were one? A cat squeezes past
the legs of the delivery boy, spaces
in the bridge railing frame a bench, plane trees,
a woman in black feeding sparrows.
No one ever takes your hand. Saturday
Vinicius lights your cigarette, Sunday
he's killed himself. You note, "the startled
eyes of the solitary sunflowers," the green patina
of the bridge, a man's smile, how the barmaid
 serves you before you say a word—this is
something, the cigarette's glow.

*

I have folded all my sweaters, placed them
squarely on the closet shelves. I lost
the egret plume that curled for years
on my desk, notebook of the hours I spent
concealed in a blind—things I've had
briefly—glimpse of a heron's red eye,
touch, the solidity of a person

before they're gone—familiar arm in sleeve,
arm-filled sleeve. Pessoa, you could
have called it *The Book of Disquietude
and Quietude*, these mounds of wool,
neat shape of a nest before winter's
unravelling—as these knitted cuffs will,
I know, but not where or when.

The quotations in a smaller font by Fernando Pessoa are from *The Book of Disquietude*, trans. Richard Zenith, (Carcanet, 1991), from selections of Pessoa's work collected in *Always Astonished*, trans. Edwin Honig (San Francisco, City Lights Books, 1991), and from *Poems of Fernando Pessoa* translated and edited by Edwin Honig and Susan M. Brown (The Ecco Press, New York, 1986).

SALLY ASHTON

I have no proof that Lisbon exists
—Fernando Pessoa

only waking dreams, like the cry of a gull
echoing in an alley or the lingering smoke
from a cigarette. Or an imaginary war
that never occurs in your homeland though
everybody bleeds. The idea of Lisbon
is like that, like listening to someone who says
No, then *Yes*, each moment changing direction,
swallows darting mid-sky. And it's summer always
in such a place that can't exist. You walk
on pavement stones slick with heat, the streets
a school of fish flashing through the city
in every direction. They rise under your feet.
This is the dream part, when the trolley turns the corner
shaking like loose change and the river
opens before you, behind you the hills—a fine
specter, glazed with unerring light.

Saudade, someone might say. Saudade is not
to be alone as I am alone, but to be apart.
Absence is proof of nothing, neither is its phantom pain.
It is a memory stolen from another language
you find you are unable to speak.

Christopher Bakken

Duet with Fernando Pessoa

At times we wish that we could disappear,
having followed too long the terrified trails of sparrows
between rafter beams and the branches of elms
—all that's been dashed upon itself
in back alleyways and coal-pits, everything I follow
on my brainless ramble through the market,
where I flatten out to fit the tatters of my wallet.
Meanwhile, the baker's fire collapses back to ash,
and the broad-chested church on the corner
absorbs all sounds not sanctioned by the rain.

When we see between things, where ether's heaving
at the border, see how the shape of the leaf, for instance,
dilates beyond contours permitted by the eye,
where underlying matter can muster beyond
the banter of books, then we see a votive geometry
known only to those versed in my Jesuit liturgy of the senses,
a new music swelling the topsails of the altar-boys' tongues.
Meanwhile, the same atomic fog,
and madmen thrash the congas of our garbage pails.

I see between things, through the narrow chinks,
through a negative space even knowing can't fill,
through a neon hum the insects master to pester us;
I surrender the hub of skin that's strung me out,
slack as an old tire, the forehead having tasted exterior
it forgot was there, my mind left back in its neoclassical urn.

Charles Cutler, Dan Mahoney & Gaby Gordon-Fox, eds.

And I'll have more wine, if that's all I think can happen,
and I'll have more wine, if life is nothing,
brimming as I drink it with gypsy ventriloquism,
noting, as I down it, my duty to the voices I must dream

Susan Baller-Shepard

Doing the Math with Fernando

> *I divide what I know. There's what I am.*
> —Fernando Pessoa

Fernando, so tortured, you couldn't speak
your mind, for the cacophony inside,
in all that dividing, what did you seek?

Who got the floor, who fell silent, too meek?
Penned by same hands, did the voices collide?
Fernando-So-Tortured, *You* couldn't speak?

Would I have loved you, or thought you a freak?
Was it a mental skid down a slick slide
in all that dividing? What did you seek

so far outside yourself? Who got a peek?
Who compromised the real you, broke you, lied,
Fernando? So tortured, you couldn't speak

the truth about loves lost, a past too bleak?
Love too dangerous a thing to be tried
in all that. Dividing, what did you seek,

as you multiplied, did you grow strong? Weak?
Reis and De Campos, a good place to hide
Fernando? So tortured, you couldn't speak.
In all that, dividing, what did *you* seek?

Charles Cutler, Dan Mahoney & Gaby Gordon-Fox, eds.

Herding Heteronyms

> *I have more than just one soul.*
> *There are more I's than I myself.*
> —Fernando Pessoa/Ricardo Reis

You're the horses we try to catch at dawn,
who shy away when the realization slides
over their skulls that we are here to rein
them in. You pull from the loops we make
with our arms, sauntering off undaunted.

Senhor, tell me, who in your herd was least
broken? Fought the bridle? Caeiro? Reis?
De Campos? Or one of your lesser ponies?
Otto, Seul, de Seabra? My friend from Lisboa
boasts, Pessoa's the best ever trotted out of Portugal!

Best ever? You're a mustang, accustomed to running loose,
caged in a pen, hammering, clamoring to get free.

Once, as a child, I came up over the rise before my sisters,
saw the horses grazing in peace, and I spooked them
so they'd scatter, to settle in the far meadow.

Sometimes horses just need a good place to be horses,
to be part of the collective, checking out their pecking
order, a chance to run, with distant boundaries;

your heteronyms desired this most, peaceful pasture
with plenty of room for all.

Aliki Barnstone

Biographical Note on Eva Victoria Perera

Eva Victoria Perera (1917–2001) was the daughter of a well-to-do jeweler and importer, Jacobo Angel, and a pianist, Sophia. Jacobo was a descendent of the Sephardic Jews who came to Thessaloniki after 1492. He met Sophia in Vienna where she was studying piano. Jacobo traveled widely and was passionate about the arts and intellectual inquiry. An unconventional man, he rejected subservient roles for women and was attracted to Sophia's strong will, humor, and musical talent. Both parents were ambitious for Eva, their only child. With their encouragement, Eva began to write and paint when she was very young. She devoted herself to poetry and considered herself only an amateur painter. Yet she was greatly influenced by the visual arts; she felt a particular kinship to the iconography of Marc Chagall.

In 1927 the Perera family hired a governess for Eva, Hope Parker, a grand-niece of the fiery Transcendentalist preacher and reformer, Theodore Parker. Fascinated by ancient Greek culture, Hope had came to Greece on a spiritual quest and as a rebellion against her New England roots. While in Thessaloniki, Hope fell in love with a charismatic Rembetis, who abandoned her when she became pregnant. When the Perera family took her in, she had an infant daughter, Ariana. As a result, Eva was trained in classical Greek and European literature, and more unusually for a Greek, in American literature. Through her mother, she heard classical music; through Parker, the underground music of Rembetika. Eva was fluent in Greek, French, Ladino (old Spanish), and English.

In 1937, Eva married Isaak Perera, a piano student of her mother's. In 1939, their daughter, Eleftheria was born. Isaak became an architect, but he was a talented pianist. The young couple lived with Eva's parents after their marriage. As Eva writes in her poem "The Piano," their home was filled with the music of Isaak and Sophia, until the family fled Thessaloniki.

When the Germans invaded Greece in 1942, Jacobo had the wherewithal to buy the immediate family false Christian identities. He took them all to the island of Andros, where they were taken in by Christian friends, the Haralambos family. Andros is a green island, full of gardens. Though all of Greece was pillaged of food by the Germans, and many starved to death, the families managed to grow and keep enough to stay alive and relatively healthy.

After the war, Eva's family returned to Thessaloniki. Nearly all their friends and relatives were dead; 50,000 Jews from the city known as "the Mother of Israel," perished in Auschwitz. Eva, Isaak, and Eleftheria found the ghosts too painful and they left Thessaloniki to settle in Athens, where Isaak established his practice. Eventually, they bought land on Andros, and built a home there; the island that had been their refuge during the war became their sanctuary from the city. Eva wrote poetry all her life, though like Cavafy she never printed her work for the public, only for her friends (who included Greece's greatest poets of the twentieth century: Seferis, Elytis, and Ritsos). After Eleftheria grew up, became an architect, and joined her father's practice, Eva spent most of her time on the island, though she traveled occasionally. She met and befriended Chagall in 1952, on his first visit to Greece. She spent her last years devoted to "growing an Eden" in her garden, where she loved to have outdoor dinner parties for her family and friends. She died among her fruit trees and flowers on

Charles Cutler, Dan Mahoney & Gaby Gordon-Fox, eds.

August 15, 2001. In 2003, a volume of her collected poems was published in Greece, edited by her daughter, Eleftheria, and her granddaughter, Sophia.

IN THE FOOTSTEPS OF A SHADOW

Introducing Eva Victoria Perera

To feign is to know oneself
—Fernando Pessoa

The summer of 2002, I was at a dinner party on the island of Serifos, talking to a mother and daughter whom I had just met. Our conversation turned to poetry, and I told them I was working on a translation of C. P. Cavafy. Eleftheria, the mother, was excited to hear about my project, and told me that she and her daughter, Sophia, were editing a volume her mother's collected poems, to be published for the first time next year. "If you love Kaváfis so much and are so deeply influenced by him," Sophia chimed in, "perhaps you would be interested in translating the poems of my grandmother, Eva Victoria Perera. There's a strange kinship between them." With some reluctance, I gave them my address in the States so that they could send the book to me when it was published. Maybe I had drunk too much, or maybe it was that Eva had died a year earlier, or that she was published by Ikaros, which also brought out the work of Seferis and Ritsos, or maybe it was curiosity. I'd never met any Greek Jews before, and Perera was a Sephardic Jew from Thessaloniki, who survived the Holocaust.

I received a copy of *Eva's Voice* in early 2003, the dark time when America was going to war with Iraq. I was getting emails from my dear friends, who had shared that auspicious table with me, saying that anti-Americanism in Greece, indeed, in all Europe, "was out of bounds." Perhaps I should, one suggested, write a letter and send it to the Greek newspapers to show the perspective of a "good American." Though I knew my friends in

Greece distinguished between me personally and my country's foreign policy, I was beside myself. The book arrived just when I needed most to hear poetry which deals with suffering and ordinary, domestic beauty. In Perera's work I heard the voice of a survivor, who feels guilt, shame, empathy, joy to be alive, to be among the lucky, while others suffer and die. As Eva's biography and work reveal, she survived through a combination of privilege and good luck. (Although there were many well-off Jews in Thessaloniki, less than four percent of the population survived; approximately 50,000 died in Auschwitz.)

Though, of course, the circumstances are crucially different, I, too, am lucky to be alive, to be able to write poems, and live among loved ones, while others are afflicted in unspeakable ways. You, too, as readers of this essay, are similarly lucky. But the privilege of life, I surmise, is mere chance, and not a reward, not controllable, not the destiny of a nationality, not evidence of grace. Those justifications might save me from living in fear, but they also might prevent me from empathizing with others, who, through accident, do not share my good fortune. *Eva's Voice* shows me a way to explore this ethical and philosophical conundrum.

Sophia had hinted at the odd affinity between Cavafy and Perera. Both poets are "poet-historians" who recount the past from the individual's perspective. Both combine an intensely personal voice with an analysis of the political. Perera wrote: "My aim is tell the stories of the past, whether ancient or twentieth century, so that they describe the now, as well. And I wish to record the voices of Greek people, Christian and Jewish, who lived through the second world war." With this statement, a trinity forms composed of Cavafy, Pessoa, and Perera. These poets are ecstatic in the word's etymological sense: each stands outside themself. Each is a dramatist or medium, even when they speak in the first person. Each in his or her own way is, as Pessoa says, "a poet who is various poets, a dramatic poet writing lyric poetry. Each mood cluster, similar to each other, will become a character with its own style and with feelings that differ from, even contradict, the feelings of the poet in his living person."

Another kinship between Pessoa and Perera is their poetics of the senses. Pessoa's Bernardo Soares proclaims, "I make holidays out of the senses." Perera's poems include all the senses, as if she like Soares had said, "Smell is a strange way of seeing." Perera does not wish to be merely a victim or to recount only horror. She wants to paint a full picture of a life, a people, and a country, and such a portrait includes beauty and love. Perera had a lifelong passion for the visual arts, and was herself an amateur painter. As such her poems are replete with color, panorama, surreal visual juxtapositions, and a desire to create with words the plasticity of the external world.

Perera draws her iconography from the work of another Holocaust survivor, Marc Chagall, a painter of witness who celebrates life. She first met Chagall in 1952 when he visited Greece. Perera records that in their conversations Chagall said, "I was accused of falling into literature.... What I call 'abstract' is something that rises spontaneously from a gamut of psychic and plastic contrasts, bringing to the picture and to the eye of the spectator realizations of the unknown objects." She replied with a quotation by Fernando Pessoa (as Alberto Caeiro), "I'm not even a poet: I see." Her poems, she said, arose from "a descent into wordlessness, into the sensory and visual, which can be as fearful and painful as it is joyful ... I regard naming the physical world as preservation and as memory. How else can we be redeemed?" In one of Perera's many homages to Chagall, "Red Picnic, 1946," she writes:

> There are no houses turned upside down.
> There's the carafe of burgundy on the red blanket
> And just a little food. A tomato. An end of bread

> So much beauty, to name it feels almost like peace,
> like sorrow to name it, too, as if my words
> could save the picture of you smiling at us....

In these lines, and in other poems, she depicts ordinary, domestic life as beautiful and strange. There is an ominous quality in the negative, "There are no houses turned upside down." As in "Day Breaks on Andros, 1944," "Picnic" implicitly asks the questions, "Why them and not me? Why do I get to have a picnic after the war, when others were taken away, their homes pillaged?" In "Andros" the speaker takes me inside just such a fear of abduction; she is "almost afraid to reassure herself" that her daughter is sleeping peacefully in the bed beside her. There's also an implied shame in that speaker and her family pose as Christians, in order to be "passed over."

Eva's Voice speaks to me from the body-politic, in a way that is similar to Pessoa's Whitmanian idea of the "People-Myself." Pessoa's Benardo Soares writes:

> To create inside myself a political state, with parties and revolutions, and I being all this, being God in the real pantheon of this People-Myself, essence and action of their bodies, of their souls, of the earth they tread and the acts they perform. To be all this and not them. Oh, well! This is still one of the dreams I cannot of fulfill. If I did, I'd die perhaps; I don't know why but one's not supposed to live after such an enormous sacrilege against God, such an enormous usurpation of the divine power to be all things.

Of course, in Soares's statement there are layers of irony and satire—he's making fun of the artist as a kind of God worshipped in the political state of his own making. Like Pessoa, Perera wants to achieve empathy and have a larger global view, and in that way be the "People-Myself." Perhaps both Pessoa and Perera show the flip side of Whitman's idea that "what I assume you shall assume / for every atom belonging to me as good belongs to you." Perera cannot help but open herself to suffering the suffering of others. But she is suspicious of power, of God, and the drive to be like God. What is the Final Solution if not "an enormous usurpation of the divine power to be all things"? If I think of others suffering, then think, "There but for the grace of God," I entertain the notion that I'm chosen for a destiny. Through her voice, Perera turns me to face the possibility of a divine void. I see that the simplest things in my daily life I enjoy by chance: taking my daughter to the park, driving a car, having water for lawns, switching on the electric lights when I prepare supper at night. For me, *Eva's Voice* brings the speaker and the reader, the self and the other together, as if she were enacting these lines by Pessoa (Álvaro de Campos):

> What I was, what I wasn't—that's all me,
> What I wanted, what I didn't, all of that gets to be me,
> What I loved, what I stopped loving—it's all the same sad
> yearning in me.

The Blue House

I can see a long way up here
where the blue house is balanced
on a bluff yellow with late summer
fields that extend to the city.

You can see me, for the door
and the windows are open to air.

I sit in a chair and hold a cup
of tea. Or is that you I see inside
and is that me, running downhill,
away from the house, on the path

lined with hip-high wheat.
Looming larger above me

the closer I come is the jumble
of buildings, a white cross atop
each sky-blue dome, the church
enclosed by Byzantine battlements.

Is that figure below the cathedral,
almost too small to see,

raising an arm toward the city
in joy? Or turning back
to wave goodbye to the house?
Why does the modest cottage

seem so isolated from town?
Why is it painted such a radiant blue?

The wood looks like the glass
of the evil eye, and the planes
aren't square, but ramshackle.
The foundation is shored up

against the hill, on the brink—
I can see the danger now.

And yet the blue house
invites us to look in, enter,
have a seat and drink
a cup of tea that tastes

too beautiful on the tongue
when you exclaim, "Ah, the view!"

The house was not blue.
My memory painted it
the color of the morning sea.
Look, out there, far from shore,

the fisherman is
disappearing in his orange boat

that floats along a gray smear
of light, marring the sapphire depths.
In the impossible pigment
is the day we have to leave

for good, to find other refuge.
No, the blue house was not

a hue in nature, sea or sky
or a precious stone.
It was a color made
by human hands, like a home.

Charles Cutler, Dan Mahoney & Gaby Gordon-Fox, eds.

Aileen Bassis

Watching A Stone

> *Sometimes, I busy myself with watching a stone,*
> *I don't begin thinking whether it feels.*
> —Fernando Pessoa

or did he chip
and chip until he split
into a pile of stones,
one different
from another as hummingbirds
and pelicans, a menagerie
of selves: the hunchbacked girl,
the doctor and the engineer,
the baron and the bookkeeper
enveloped in a mystery of mustaches
and eyeglasses, a buttoned coat,
a buckle and a cane and when
one self blinked
another coughed
and his pen itched
to scratch more words
linked like clockwork
gears turning with a click.

Charles Bernstein

Autopsychographia

    after Fernando Pessoa

Poets are fakers
Whose faking is so real
They even fake the pain
They truly feel
And for those of us so well read
Those read pains feel O, so swell
Not the poets' double header
But the not of the neither
And so the wheels go whack
Ensnaring our logical part
In the train wreck
Called the human heart

    1 April 1931

Charles Cutler, Dan Mahoney & Gaby Gordon-Fox, eds.

At Pessoa's Grave

I'm not me
nor you you
neither we we
but all's found
in them's they

David Biespiel

Supremo Fernando

When happy, I felt haunted as a passerby, obscene
And absolute, as if my memory were oblivious to the quaint
    lessons
I took through the useless streets—sincerity, tedium,
Comfort, or whatever skittery, moonlit gloom
Overtook, some enduring incandescence I was too weary to
    marvel at.
Then, the science of unknowns brought joy and belief—
And the sketchy treatments I made of that, what were they but
    a rip-off
Of monotony, a nightmare of splendor? What other conclusion
But to scold myself for how I existed? Then, to reciprocate with
Base sensations I scraped or smoked out from my unfaithful
    heart.
I didn't know who I was the advent of. At once invalid
Or else no more than a throb of a body, the simplest grunt.
If there was a limit to what I could steal, an invisible horizon
To pack the wagon for, I'd have done it. But, could I pawn
Another voice onto this unbearable self? What is left to adapt?

Charles Cutler, Dan Mahoney & Gaby Gordon-Fox, eds.

NOAH BLAUSTEIN

Flea/New House/Mutated Line of Pessoa's

The new owners unroll their carpet of gold
shag before me, their field of late fall
corn, of wheat, of Russian Tumbleweed, of dried
witch's hair (*convolvulaceae*). I am this house's
first flea brought in by the new dog,
this house's first miniature gazelle,
obsidian antelope, ebony kangaroo,
beauty's shadow sent by gods
to rule over dust mites, to populate
this carpet, this plain and tundra, with blood
suckers, vectors, cathedrals of sloughed
skin. I am prince of the red welt, overlord
of minutiae, humility's servant, the itch
tonight next to the husband's belly button
(the trailhead to the treasure trail)
as his wife goes down on him
in celebration of ownership,
in celebration of their new home.

Doug Bolling

For Pessoa
for Fernando Pessoa

You who scorned greatness
and now live in its shrine
like a remote god behind
a veiled face,

like a cloud that flees
all orchestrations of
fixed lines drawn in a sky
by hierophants or
busy fools or
pedants on a stool.

You who chose the far end
of the cave where shadows tell
only of themselves and leave
their shapes behind
moment by moment.

You who scorned Plato's timeless
icons blinding with a light
this world has never seen
or touched
or smelled.

But you, Fernando Pessoa,
how did you foresee such

breakage in the myths,
such dismantling of epistemes
even Derrida, even Foucault
would be proud to claim.

You the chooser of a thousand
coats discarding and plucking
anew as drowsy afternoons
sang their witchery,
as your pen flowed on
searching not for absolutes
but for the crossroads
of spaces and times
just there,
just themselves.

You who poked out the soul
they assigned you
and dropped it almost
casually
in a bag
for others to track
like divers descending
to claim the impossible
treasure, anything to
prove worth of
such emptiness
full of marvels.

JOHN BRADLEY

Footnote to a Line by Pessoa

"I want to fly and fall from up high!" (1)

(1) In Charles Lindberg's diary, composed after his transatlantic flight, he said that to stay awake in the *Spirit of St. Louis* he recited "lines from that great Portuguese poet what's-his-name." No doubt he was referring to Fernando Pessoa's "Salutation to Walt Whitman," by Álvaro de Campos. Perhaps the very line above. Some think, however, that this diary entry was meant as a challenge to those who later claimed that Lindberg recited "99 Bottles of Beer on the Wall" during the flight. The implication being, of course, that the beer was German, a reference to Lindberg's admiration of Nazi beer. Still other critics have argued that this entry was not written by Lindberg, but inserted into Lindberg's diary by Brendan Gill, a friend of Lindberg's but also an admirer of Pessoa. If true, perhaps Gill meant it as a tribute to Walt Whitman, though friends of Gill insist that he thought Whitman's poetry "made Longfellow look good." Still others believe Lindberg's diary was ghostwritten by his wife, Anne Morrow, and her "Portuguese" reference was to Elizabeth Barrett Browning's *Sonnets from the Portuguese.* But a disgruntled copy editor, who detested sonnets, changed the line so it alluded to the free verse of Pessoa. The most intriguing account of the Lindbergh-Pessoa connection, however, comes from a member of Lindberg's ground crew, a certain L. Hampton Moon. In an interview given in a Long Island tavern, Moon disclosed that an unknown person appeared at the airstrip shortly before Lindbergh's takeoff and paid Moon to place a book by Pessoa (though Moon used the name "Pizarro,"

perhaps a combination of "Pessoa" and "Álvaro"?) in the cockpit of the *Spirit of St. Louis*. Moon, though finding the request rather odd, didn't ask any question as he wanted the money to acquire a rare boomerang for his collection. Years later, when Moon questioned Lindbergh about the incident, Lindberg would only say, "I tossed the torn-out pages and let the winds take them where they would." A further complication to the story takes us to the Toledo Museum of Modern Art. There in 1989, I came across a framed page, one having suffered intense salt water and sun damage. From Pessoa's "Salutation to Walt Whitman," it was identical to page 98 of *Another Republic: 17 European & South American Writers*, edited by Charles Simic and Mark Strand (which includes four Pessoa poems translated by Edwin Honig). The anonymous "artist" who framed this found page added a footnote to the line "I want to fly and fall from way up high!" That footnote read: "(1) Imagine falling from 'way up high' and not remember member embering." When contacted recently, the Toledo Museum staff could find no record of the Pessoa page ever appearing in the museum.

How to Float

> *Fernando Pessoa, strictly speaking, does not exist.*
> —Álvaro de Campos

On the street of countless fragments, he testifies with each step: Here there is no one to look at, no one looking, no one to look for, nothing to know.

Let your head, adrift after falling, drop back and empty. Even if the Dead Sea is not dead and not a sea, lie back and try to relax. Tilt your chin toward the Gulf of Mexico, keeping just offshore.

That's why the black-knotted tie, the newspaper under his left arm, back foot, coming forward, beginning to blur, a sign of what's to come.

Some humans float without finding equilibrium, as though an angel full of oxygen. Some rotate into a vertical position as though 30 miles from a horizontal position. Your body movements will rotate somebody on land.

The dutiful folded coat, how it carries itself with exhausted resignation, leaning upon the arm of someone who wears such clothing to remain invisible.

Underwater you hear 10 times: You're not the noises of your skull. Suckerfish bypass themselves for about 20 seconds. Stay alive by vibrating your chest, with no idea how to drink in the night.

The right hand, further blurred, must be free at all times to hush the man with the loud cigar, brush the sleeve of the woman with ink scalding her fingertips.

Some dolphins will surrender to the fierce noises in your legs. If you're human, eventually you will begin to rub your skull. The strangest thing, not to drown in biomechanics and whale frequencies.

Note the glasses, how they evoke accountant, midnight scholar of Roman law, sewer-cover aficionado; hear his backdraft mutter, *Fernando António Nogueira Pessoa once passed this way through.*

Just keep telling yourself: Not dying can be surreal.

Jenny Browne

Be Plural Like the Universe!
—Fernando Pessoa

Today the brain a scatter-graph of slipped coordinates
and I failed geometry, plum gave up
on astrology when I learned it was mostly math.

The only pattern out there is in the finger of a man
tapping telephone buttons on air, figuring the constellation
of a connection he once knew by heart.

Disappointment a clear sky with too much
dead light below to name stars. So what
if we all just insist our hearts plural want out

of the chorus, tired of enunciating to the universe of cough,
shuffle and sigh. Pessoa once wrote to a friend *I have been
on the move several years now in order to collect ways of feeling.*

Mrs. Whittier, who turns 103 on Tuesday, says *maybe
if we all just wake up each day a little less angry.*
Maybe.

After the field trip a child supposes *If the people who saw us
didn't know we were a school, they might think
we were a mighty family.*

Charles Cutler, Dan Mahoney & Gaby Gordon-Fox, eds.

I think the world. Maybe if they didn't see how
we franchise cruelty and chew silently
in our plastic corners, they might mistake us

for a mighty family too. I used to think I knew
who we and they were for sure. Pessoa also wrote
Let me have more wine, life is nothing.

Sometimes I ask rooms full of children, *Have you ever
gone inside your poems?* One boy says you would have to
be small, very very small. That moment I hate most

all the things I've forgotten, the feeling of being
        so many others, small and learning
how to spell *February* or *lightning.*

Christopher Buckley

I Too Am Not a Keeper of Sheep: Variation on a Theme by Pessoa

> *There's metaphysics enough in not thinking about anything.*
> —Fernando Pessoa

What's still following me around these days, I don't know—
    at least
it isn't self pity, a bum with a bitter cup of coffee
from the convenience store

mumbling next to me on the bench, for each evening I'm
    comforted,
sitting here, thinking backwards, watching as those
gauzy abstractions of my youth

with their berets and French unfiltered cigarettes and dogma
are devoured like Pharaoh's army by the great grey
jawbones of the sea as the fog advances.

And it's not the miasma of middle age, not unless I'm going
to live to 116. Done with that, I still take a great delight
in breaking off a bright armful of gladioli

from the abandoned beds by the library—a little defiance
to everything.... For meaning, I drift back
as far as the reeds and river bed,

thumb through my old Geography to what we called
Asia Minor, where it could just as easily have been
my atoms as Aristotle's, suspended

in the dust above an Aegean port, glimmering like anything
for sale. How I wandered through the aethers
to arrive here can only be explained

by the chaotic logic of matter as it reorganizes itself, the spin
a little light puts on it all. However, thinking alone
has, it seems, never accounted for much

happiness. Why, if there is a God overlooking the shrubs,
should He be concerned with me, obstinate and
agnostic as I've grown ever since

the Dodgers left Brooklyn, and that idiot Timmy Armour
tossed my Wilson Bob Feller mitt by the classroom
door after school for any unconscionable kid

to steal, and who, 46 years later, has yet to apologize or
make restitution, if such could possibly be made
for that supple sun yellow steer hide

glove that snagged the visible and invisible whistling by
my ear at Third. It was the singular illumination
of my sullen youth, the only unyielding

source beyond the truthless, confabulated tales of parochial
    school.
If I have a soul, there is only a string now holding it
down as I float here on the cliff

above the Pacific, like the lantana or sea vetch at the mercy
of any change in wind. So how, in their insolence
and apostasy, could I not admire

the industrial brotherhood of crows just over my shoulder,
    their fearlessness
before the blue, as they sit in the coral tree,
blossoms flaming all around them,

redeemed in their own darkness? If we come back, I wouldn't
    want
to be one of them—every day just a day
away from starving, trying

to pick the pocket of circumstance, never sure of the next crust.
Nothing's worth giving up knowing that I don't
know, the plain improbability of Life

Ever After, as we were made to pray. Oxygen,
for instance, is an implicit theology—the proof
is in continuing to breathe,

in any tree drawing up water wordlessly, answering its own
prayer. Whatever thoughts I have, I'm happy
to let them wander away like clouds,

beyond explanation—like a few sheep grazing aimlessly
downhill toward the sea, where there is still more
than enough mystery to go around.

Midnight Walk
after Pessoa

Most nights I can see all the universe
that's available from the mesa
and the western cliffs. This is everything
I will ever have—glimmering strands
upon which we've hung our theories …
Even the sea that holds their light
grudgingly gives it back,
                           and even
the fish washed up on shore,
their eyes filled with the sky.
Fog seeps in erasing the magnolia
and acacia, leaf by leaf—likewise,
I am content to walk about in anonymity,
whistling "My Blue Heaven" or one
or another of my father's '40s or '50s tunes
still washing unconsciously around in my brain,
just as I did as a boy, wondering
about nothing, about every molecule
under the sky.
               Still, nothing stops me
thinking. I continue to sort through
the abraded artifacts, the nuts and bolts
of birth waiting to surface like rust,
like sea salt through my pores,
and start perhaps, somewhere
all over again …

Space, they tell us
now, is not eternal—there is a curtain
beyond which, beyond which ...
and if you take up that line of thought
you could say God has more work left to do.
These clouds for instance, so many
grey washcloths hung on the horizon line,
are rinsed of any suggestion—I feel emptied
just looking at them, as though I'd known
the bottom line about hope all along.
Stopping here on the breakwater,
my heart gives up its tug of war
with the stars, the wind leaving
rope burns in my hands....

Sue D. Burton

A Love Letter to Álvaro De Campos

Dear Álvaro—you figment, you fragment, you
noncommit—where have you been?
Not at your window ... no letter for weeks.
*Your absence (and you, Álvaro de Campos,
you ...) always makes me suffer....*

Keats is out there writing Fanny Brawne, *You
have absorb'd me ... I cannot breathe
without you.* Pessoa is out there writing
Ophelia Queiroz, *How constantly, insanely
I've missed you.* And you?—holed up
in Pessoa's flat, mailing me
smoke rings, *All love letters
are ridiculous.*

So. Tell me: am I real? Or am I nothing
but a whim—*a little Ophelia
of your own?*
You were mean to the
flesh-and-blood Ophelia, calling her
Pessoa's hook. Crochet, busy work.
You put the zed to her all right.
And the letters you write me? Loops
of string? An excuse to slink
into your room to *feel all things*
propped at your desk.

Well, Álvaro, you were a better
read in your Whitmanic phase. Go put
this in your 'Sensationalist Manifesto'—it is I
(S. Birria, remember me?) who *has*
a heart! Who feels to the core!
Yet, yet ...
something wrong about me
which my constitution will either conquer
or give way to—

Do not show my letters to Pessoa. Stop
invading my dreams. And keep your kisser off
my Tarot cards.

Enough of this!—I am not strong enough
to be weaned—

Álvaro, in truth, I too write as an excuse
to be alone, *the universal sea, the longing,*
away from people and their selves
pressing upon me.
I am sitting in the back room.
But whose room, whose fancy?—whose
objects teeter on shelves, exuding identity—
cups the color of canary, plates
heavy with hunger.
Álvaro, I write as an excuse to be.
But such a tawdry present. *Tomorrow*
I too will vanish from the Rua da Prata....

WILLIAM CARPENTER

Clone
for J. A.

Free man in a free country, your family off to New York
for Passover, long winter through, cold war expired,
love stabilized for the time being, nothing to die for,

alone; this might be a good time to make your clone.
A snip from your useless nipple, a quick trip to Scotland
a borrowed or rented ewe, and you will be two

an old and a new you, and just in time too. Death has
been stalking you. No basset hound face, no cold feet
from standing on the shore of time, no hernia

poking through. Your sins are forgiven you. The time
you nearly mated with a ewe, in the Holmgrens' barn, you
next in line, then you were called for supper, lamb stew.

Everyone got some but you. Down in New York, they leave a chair
empty for you, horseradish, marror, salt bread of captivity too,
but you're not alone, you're home, you're grilling a pork chop

with your clone. On this night like no others. You pig. You
should be on your knees. Instead, you are watching *The Simpsons*
on TV. You lose. You are a Pharisee. Your only religion is the news.

Consider the lamb of God—King, man and Jew—He was
     cloned too,
using a pure human female instead of the usual ewe.
Your clone will outdistance you. He will outlive and outdo.

He will know every fact that you knew. He will watch
what you smoke and you chew. He will breathe the same air
as you do. He'll have false buried memories of you. You'll
need an attorney or two. When he grows up he could sue.

Albino Carrillo

Pessoa Crosses the Atlantic to Meet Some North Americans

Pessoa Schmessoa
 —Allen Ginsberg, from "Salutations to Fernando Pessoa"

Fernando Pessoa crosses the Atlantic and it's dark,
dark like the river Styx. In the distance
he sees the last lights, the rockets, the bright flares
of the Titanic. It's before radio. Somehow, though,
he knows that Leonardo DiCaprio is freezing in the cold
still water, and that Kate Winslet is floating
like an angel above him on piece of bulkhead.
It's unlike Melville, who imagined the ocean to be like a prairie,
who imagined the One Eye of the Oversoul projecting itself
    out of the depths.
Like a comet from darker skies, major poetry journals acclaim
    his arrival: for
one critic, he's like the hysterical, drug-soaked Poe,
and for another, he reads like a militant Christopher Smart
    without Jeoffry the cat.
Still, there is no sense of time on his passage,
but there are fellows in New England practicing a kind
of spiritual folk magic after all, and the docks are still thick
with poisonous intrigue, the slap of chains and rope.
The crisis begins with postmodernism,
the crisis begins with the colonial instinct he carries, they say.

So in desperation he meets every gang-plank by begging,
"*Have you seen my men, have you seen my ships?*"

Pessoa crosses the Ohio and it's green,
slimy with gasoline. By this time he's been waiting
for hours to cross into the great Heartland,
riding a modern coal barge all the way to St. Louis.
He knows the old Greybeard is there, singing
long flat songs in an accent he doesn't know.
You see, the lobstermen of Nantucket and the catfish farmers
in Louisiana know they have options—traps, tools, and
a good road to make a living, the slap of brotherhood.
Stuck with his poetry he toughs it out along the great vein
of North American might until March, unable to sail,
but able to fish the muddy waters for fish he never imagined,
red-gilled things that writhe in the fire,
thick-finned things that taste like so much salt.
There's a point in the story when Pessoa
reaches San Francisco, where the steel ships are the size of
castles and the dreary Japanese Pacific awaits him. But now,
this is America, or as you would say,
North America, and because of Whitman
he's mistaken for a Beatnik or even a later day
Essene who might make soap near the sea.
I can't help it if Richard Henry Dana is there with him,
barefoot, selling seal hides in the harbor from a sloop.
In the pseudo-romantic light of the bay, it's just a story.

Roberto Christiano

Sometimes It Is Necessary to Be Someone Else

Fernando Pessoa had no life.
He was a clerk who did translations of business documents.
He wasn't known among the literati or even at the local cafe.
But Alberto Caeiro, Ricardo Reis, and Álvaro de Campos had
    lives.
Alberto was the rude Zen country boy who wrote about daisies
    and sheep,
Ricardo, the formally educated doctor and classicist,
Álvaro, the bisexual naval engineer who traveled to the Orient
and contemplated the existential nature of a cold.
Instead of one life Pessoa acted out 72.

I was also an actor.
It took up all of my life.
Instead of loves I had parts with love.
There was always love onstage.
In Persephone, I played 22 characters,
most of them in love and by extension miserable.
A few got to die onstage.

Pessoa died a virgin,
but Ricardo wrote about amorous odes to Lydia and others,
while Álvaro de Campos longed to have sex with Walt Whitman
    aboard a ship—

like many Portuguese he had to have the sea in order to do
 anything.

I had sex for the first time in my forties.
I was tired of being a Catholic
and doing fake sex scenes in student films
I played a whore in Brecht on Brecht.

Pessoa was five when he lost his father to tuberculosis
and his brother Jorge died in infancy.
The next year he created his first heteronym, Chevalier de Pas.
He grew up small and thin and learned to hide behind his glasses
 and mustache.

I came to writing late.
I gave up my contacts, hair rinse, and flat stomach.
Even though I am Portuguese,
I assumed a Spanish heteronym.
It was still too hard to be myself.

Pessoa published next to nothing in his lifetime.
Each year he emerges out of the darkness
as someone we do not know.

Each year I am still learning who I am.

The Terror of Wrestling the Masked Miguel Torquiero While Eating Baked Bread in Brazil

> *Poetry is an incurable and contagious disease.*
> —Don Quixote

You're hidden in the dark
saying all these bad things
that you normally wouldn't
have the nerve to say—
only there is this partition
dotted with tiny holes
and light streaming out
from behind them
like the grace of God.
The partition gives you strength,
but you haven't been to confession
in light years, and now,
when you do go
it's face to face.
Even when you were younger
and used the partition—
well, that wasn't very pleasant.
Then, there was terror
and it's not like terror.

Maybe it's like fighting with an angel.
You get in some good Old Testament action
(Jacob, God, Israel, etc.),
and you know you like that.
The title "Wrestling With"
comes to mind, but there is already
a guide to gay spirituality called that
so maybe you should skip it.
But this reminds you of the time you stopped
using your pseudonym Miguel Torquiero
because you were no longer ashamed
of writing erotic poems about men.
You in essence killed Miguel Torquiero.
Maybe it's like killing your pseudonym.
You could use the title:
The Death of Miguel Torquiero.
(But then again maybe it's not like that either.)

Maybe it's like baking bread
or planting four-o'clocks from seed,
only baking and gardening are boring.
Besides, gardening reminds you of eating,
which in turns reminds you of sex,
and while it's similar to sex,
it's not exactly like sex.

Maybe it's like survival—
like a raft off the *Titanic*,
or a safari through the Amazon of Brazil

In the Footsteps of a Shadow

where it's only you and the native guide,
who says his name is Álvaro de Campos,
and even though you are Portuguese,
you don't speak his tribal tongue.

Well maybe, but perhaps
it's more like a warm day in winter
or a lost day at the races
or an outlet or an inlet
or a song or a gong.

A gong?

Enough.

It's like what it is.

Charles Cutler, Dan Mahoney & Gaby Gordon-Fox, eds.

Frank Christmas

Caeiro Would Hold

that a poem might be made of it,
epiphanies and all: precious
and common, a tribute to
nature, a capital N. Take the rock:
for its hardness we praise it
(solid citizen!) as far as we can
throw it. Or the star: for its
twinkle (beacon of light!)
upon which the dimmest
and blindest cast wishes
at night, I among them:
am blind without glasses,
hiding by day like a bat
from the sun (it shimmers!).
The moon is another matter.
Take the moon: for the man
inside (it's a fairy tale, mostly),
for the men on the surface
(their golf game improves),
for the moonshine beams (good
for travel, or drinking), for the
cheese that it's made of (more
fairy tales, mostly), for the—
hell, take the moon for the
cow that jumps over it.
Take the moon and the rock
and the star, take them all

but don't take my word. Before them
I'm blind. See for yourself:
write a brief poem whose aim
is improvement. If you like
put on glasses but don't think
there's much to say about
water. Take lakes: their calm
surface (still waters!) or
rivers that flow, mountains
that tower, take meadows
—they roll. In his own fatigued
way, Caeiro would hold that
a poem might be made of them.

Charles Cutler, Dan Mahoney & Gaby Gordon-Fox, eds.

ALEX CIGALE

The Spirit of Lindbergh

Seeking escape he hurled himself again
and again against the sky. Complete loss
of all conscious connection with the past.

Reaching all the way back to his childhood
his chronic restlessness, fear of facing
himself, then the unmourned loss of his son.

*You can't write about Charles without writing
about me.* Filled with love for her husband,
the differences between man and wife.

Ever on the alert for dangers
he tried to predict the unpredictable:
insults in the press, democracy's decline.

The "omitted material" revealed:
*A few Jews add strength and character
to a country, too many create chaos....*

A pressing sea of yellow, brown, and black.
(*Reader's Digest*, 1939). Late in life
a one-man conservation commando corps

dropping from the skies wherever species
were endangered, indigenous people threatened
by change. He changed, lent his name to the cause.

Dying from cancer on Maui, his last days
meticulously planning his own funeral
he picked the reading, chose the inscription,

the typeface for his tombstone, had his grave
dug to precise specifications and saw
to it that his death certificate was signed.

Every line was filled in except the date.

Charles Cutler, Dan Mahoney & Gaby Gordon-Fox, eds.

LEONARD CIRINO

Two from Ricardo Reis, The Sad Epicurean

The Sun Comes Up and Looks at Me

The sun comes up and looks at me.
The chill leaves the air, grasses stir.
Surely life is as real as nature.

But then it sets, the moon rises
And causes me doubt. Reflection
Is more real than life.

I water the orchard in the full light
Of evening, dim shadows of noon.

How the fruit gleams, so ripe with sugar,
Sweet in the flesh, tart by the pit.

The Woods Are Dark

I write what I don't know.
It is a sacred place, the spot
That wants nothing more
Than to hear myself think
And talk as a man would
When he goes to the fields
And works the soil.

I work the words
That have given me
Wood, the world
With many shades.

Charles Cutler, Dan Mahoney & Gaby Gordon-Fox, eds.

Contemplating *The Keeper of Sheep* by the Unwitting Master, Alberto Caeiro

1

Whatever it is, a flower or a piece of shit,
it should fill the soul with sorrow or joy,
or something like contemplating mystery.

Outliving sadness is one of those things, as it is
a kind of courage or judgment, a sorrow
that leads to conclusion, natural and right.

Poetry is not my ambition, but simply one way
of staying by myself in a world of awful things
and the grandiose thoughts they expose.

It may be rain or a small, neutered lamb,
but all things compose themselves in a kind
of song, relative to their own and other selves.

As many things that can be happy are scattered
across my mind, which is like a meadow
at the beginning of autumn, just starting to die.

Hearing my ideas instead of seeing or feeling them,
begins to form an automatic way of explaining,
why I believe and why I don't, the rest of the world.

I can give you sunshine, or rain if darkness is needed.
That way you get little glimpses of what life is like
for someone other than your servant self.

And even if I did keep sheep, which I've never been good at,
I'd follow the strays into gullies and dark places
light doesn't enter, just to observe the most precious life.

2

To say I love the natural world would be an expression
of what I think. But thinking is only a temporary truth
what if I saw the maggots eating carrion?

To go outside on a cloudless night and see the quarter moon
is true metaphysics. Under its light I don't think of much else—
well, maybe the legs and hips of that woman I noticed today.

And what if I do have opinions about God and creation?
Cause and effect, free will or fate? From moment to moment
my ideas change—like a child asked, *ice cream or soda?*

And because the sea has no religion it doesn't know
wrong from right. It just moves back and forth
when the winds come up and knock hell out of the boats.

Looking at things the way they appear teaches us
belief. But to question the meaning of the universe?
Now there's a thought that can lead to delusion.

If we obey God do we think we know more about Him
than we do the world? All living turns into a prayer
that I learn to listen every moment.

God? Who's that? Some concept of a bushy-haired man
with a long white beard? Give me stars, the moon, trees,
rivers, the sea. Even the open road will do in these times.

3

I see meanings in things that aren't there.
It's my particular form of dementia that wind
and stones speak. It's my problem, not yours.

If something is more beautiful than something else
it is only my opinion. When I go into a grove
of redwoods each one has its individual nature.

The Eel River is one of the few major rivers that flows
north on our continent. This makes it unusual, but not
necessarily beautiful. Yet, it belongs to no one.

I can understand how someone owns his body
or even his house, which is bad enough. But to say
the natural world belongs to humankind is a sin.

The redwoods don't make the locals think of much—
maybe eternity if they're lucky. They simply live
here, next to us, by the rivers, in the natural world.

4

Someone might say, *I know how to see.* But to see
things for what they really are is a musical talent.
The trick is to unlearn what we have always named them.

To exist spontaneously and learn how not to reflect.
This is a lesson I don't know. How can a man who occupies
so much time with thought even begin to notice the sunrise?

What good is the sunrise to a different man who is so involved
with his emotions and himself that he has no time to reflect?
The moon rises and disappears. Few people ever really care.

I have questions about worship. Some people have faith in ideas
that are doubtful. Others are obsessed with material objects:
we live for economics and not economy.

Everything in the world is natural, but
reality doesn't exist. There is nothing total
to which all this belongs. Things can't touch.

Startled at this epiphany I closed the book. And how
did this happen without making contact? The world is
a marvelous place. I know because I don't know anything.

Charles Cutler, Dan Mahoney & Gaby Gordon-Fox, eds.

Portrait of Fernando Pessoa

His hands like sparrows,
alternately fidget and then
hush, his mind alive with
fado and the accordion's monkey,
his mouth rushing
to another cognac, bored
with reason and metaphysics, wanting only
the sun on the meadow,
the woman upstairs to
begin her piano,
his acquaintance to visit the
tobacconist, and the
shopkeeper to wave,
amused that Fernando
would sit by the window all
day, waiting for something to happen
while he smoked without peace, in
a silence he hoped would remove
him from the world.

BILLY COLLINS

The Day After Tomorrow

If I had to pick a favorite
from the four heteronyms of Fernando Pessoa, it
would have to be Álvaro de Campos,
cast in the role of the Jaded Sensationist.

This morning nothing much is going on,
just the cat re-curling herself on a chair and the
tea water coming to a boil—
a scene Álvaro would have found entirely sufficient,

he who failed to start or finish anything, who
prefers the window
to the door, tomorrow to today
or better still, the day after tomorrow,

that citadel of stillness, unspoiled
by ambition or labor, unblemished even by a
hand lowering a needle onto a record
or moving a deck chair to a place in the sun.

Yes, I like the dreamy Pessoa
who avoids streetcars and markets,
and who, like the snowflake, barely exists at all, but
that's not to say I don't care for the others.

Right now, out my back window,
all four Pessoas are chasing one another

around a big tree, holding on to their hats, each one
somehow dressed more outlandishly

than the others. Above them a pale sky,
white clouds moving like sailboats over Portugal. I can see it all
from my couch where
I'm playing a few sad tunes on the piccolo.

Meanwhile, the tea water has boiled away,
and the crown of flames is working on the kettle, and the cat has
moved to another spot.
She loves the unmade bed, the mountainous sheets.

Craig Czury

from *Book of Disquiet*: Deep Calls To Deep

5[91]

> *I often find myself mesmerized by Senhor Vasques. What does this man represent to me beyond the chance inconvenience of his being master of my time ... So why do I think about him so much? Is he a symbol? A motive force?*

Because I travel so much and because I once heard that there are seven standard facial types that we're all a variation of I see you everywhere. Is it only embarrassment that prevents me from coming up to you and saying, *Hey!* and giving you a great long-lost hug?

2/7/06

3[81]

> ... *I imagined myself free forever of Rua dos Douradores, of my boss Vasques, of Moreira the book-keeper, of all the other employees, the errand boy, even the cat.... Freedom would mean rest, artistic achievement, the intellectual fulfillment of my being,... But suddenly, even as I imagined this (during the brief holiday afforded by my lunch break), a feeling of displeasure into the dream: Yes, I would be sad.... Vasques, Moreira the book-keeper, Borges the cashier, all the lads, the cheery boy who takes the letters to the post office, the errand boy, the friendly cat—they have all become part of my life. I could never leave all that behind....*

Thoughts that keep me tethered to home:
   All the nagging, unfinished chores:
   drywall plaster and paint.
   seal and cement basement walls.
   categorize boxes in my studio
   what to shelve, box for archives, throw away.
   insulate attic.
H. becomes Emily Dickinson when I'm gone for days.
She becomes Virginia Woolf when I'm gone for weeks.
She becomes Gertrude Stein when I'm gone for months.
Sequestered in her room and writing ... lonely, lone, hermetic.
We're coming to agreement that fifteen years just may be enough.
It was my idea at first, but she's come around to seeing it too.
We slow-dance more in the kitchen while I'm cooking.
We hold each other tighter when we sleep.

                                                      2/4/06

Jon Davis (as Chuck Calebrese)
Commencement Address

> *However ...*
> —Professor Irwin Corey

It is a great & misbegotten pleasure
to be wilting here among you,
the sandwashed sons & daughters
of the recently merged, here
in the torpor, in the kindled rash
of August, along the sand-raddled
banks of the Gitahoolie, that nameless,
time-encrusted squiggle
on the overburdened maps.
Where the stickleback curls
in its bubble nest. Where the lammergeier
cribs a knockwurst from the bagelman.
Where the bagelman creeps along the focaccia
like a budgerigar on fire. Let me begin
with a brief synopsis of the challenge
that lies ahead for you, the Institute's
neotonous & yet gravid class of 2000.
First, there is the Formica of the Lost,
little-explored, but formidable
nonetheless. Then, in rapid
succession: The Festival of Poor Reception;
the tangled sweathog by the macramé;
the callous preacher in the bean dip; the grifter
with the head of a calabash. And

Charles Cutler, Dan Mahoney & Gaby Gordon-Fox, eds.

the hoarse admonishments: You call this
an airline. You call this a fortuitous
Afghani. The dreamers have whelped
the bailiwick. They've catapulted the melons.
They've capitulated by the squeezebox.
Ladies & gentlemen, here
are your craven muskox. Here are your
cantilevered hooligans. All this, my children—
the cartoon vixens, the crenelated wombats,
the swarthy G-Men & their pathogenic
G-wives—all this, my children—
from here to the dimpled horizon, from
here to the quadruple bypass, from the crapulent
to the untested, from the fortuitous masqueraders
to the fortitudes masquerading
as vipers—all this, my children, will someday—
bring the knockwurst! bring the jalapeno dip!—
will someday—hail the Coptic savants!—be yours.
Thank you my synthesized drummers, thank you
my husky *baby, babies*. And thank you
my extrinsic cadavers, my mutton cravers, my
greedy unwashed, my halfwit Carpathian sidekicks.
Today is an important day in your lives,
in your parents' lives, in the lives of your country.
Today is a grievous finicula, a cavernous
sinkhole, an encrypted fiction. Today, well,
we all know what today is. It is, of course,
a severed hand on the chifferobe, a slandered
politician weeping in the vestibule. We all know,

each of us, what today truly is:
a flatulent gaucho, a convex
caravan, a fortuitous affliction,
a sweat-drenched Caravaggio, a garrisoned
battalion of lunchboxes. Thank you
for this opportunity to thwart
your earnest hopes. Go forth then
with your magisterial airs,
with your bloody slipknots. Go forth
then, newly inducted into the splendor.
Go forth benighted ones. I think
I speak for everyone here—your impoverished
benefactors, your goat-bearded
mentors, your avid creditors.
We already anticipate
the gnarled vexations, the avarice
and spleen of your defibrillated careers.

Jon Davis

Notes to the Haitian Poems of Madeleine Du Plessix

[1] Here, the language uncharacteristically suggests a world outside of language yet touched by language, as a boot might suggest a foot, as a night might discriminate a dawn. Contemporary thinkers, Madeleine du Plessix included, realize the futility in this proposition. No foot. No dawn. Emptiness, as the author stated in more than one of her "philosophical assays," *is its own petard.*

[2] The cryptographical sense with which the author has imbued this passage is, of course, *sui generis*, and should be ignored at the reader's peril.

[3] Translation: "She floats on language as water floats on a raft."

[4] Though poorly rendered, the author intends here the international symbol meaning "crosswalk." (Scrawled marginalia: "this emblematic sign is a kind of attenuated language, neither oral, nor written—unsound(ed)").

[5] Here, she claims to have "caught a tremendous fish." Roy Jones reports a certain skepticism among the guides at Harry's Bait Shack. [Note: Autobiographical readings were anathema to the author, especially after her "Junk Bond Sequence" of the 1980s.]

[6] This, authorities suggest, should be passed over in silence.

⁷See note 6.

⁸The oppressed in Haiti have a word for this phenomenon. Linguists believe the word is of West African origin, though little else is known.

⁹The Russian aristocracy provided the model for this practice when they chose to speak in French. For the czars, the language's foreignness must have had, du Plessix believed, "both a lurid, depraved quality and a pleasing unintelligibility."

¹⁰Should read "scared," not "sacred." (See uncorrected proofs and manuscripts collected at the Beineke Rare Book Library.)

¹¹"When the silken dragon was inflated and carried by the residents through the dirt streets," she noted in her journals, "the town took on a mythical quality that had not been present."

¹²Text here is illegible. Originally thought to be a list of items the author planned to purchase and a note—"Bearded oysters. Menhaden. Paper bags. Steak. Arugula. Mayo. Visit quaint wooden church," a computer analysis suggests the following match: "Boarded windows. Men with paper bags sitting long-legged and lazy on the wooden porch—" Authorities cite photos that show a neighboring abandoned building much like the one described.

¹³It was during this trip to Haiti that the author became enamored of what she called "her negritude." Biographers, citing her French/Irish ancestry, remain baffled by this statement.

[14] Most scholars believe that *santeria* rituals, including, perhaps, the accidental ingestion of the poisonous *Datura*, were the "cause" of her feverishness. Others suggest she was spurned by a local fisherman, her bold advances taken, instead, as threats.

[15] Her journal entry for July 13 of the same year: "Passionate lovemaking with Andre M. on beach south of the cottage."

[16] Her attraction to the mysterious woman (some think the daughter of a Haitian sugar-cane mogul) referred to only as S. would later create "problems" for the local authorities, according to police reports.

[17] Her journal entry for July 15: "Passionate lovemaking with S. on the beach south of the cottage."

[18] Following the supposed method of Gertrude Stein, the author began "encoding" certain aspects of her sexual life. Scholars note the surfeit of references to flowers, pistils, and stamens (often, perhaps humorously, *sous rature*), and to being "pollen-drunk." Her shopping lists become increasingly more obtuse and—to her redactors—intriguing during this period.

[19] Marginalia: "No, no, no, no, no! This will not do!" Handwriting experts have long maintained that these comments are in the handwriting of the mysterious S. Biographers continue to insist that S. was simply a dramatic enactment of the author's "divided self."

[20] Her journal entry for August 3: "Martinis on the Hotel Continental lawn with S. Long conversation about her childhood, so alien to my own. I was struck at how different a person I might be had I grown up in Haiti."

[21] Increasingly, the author refers to the prejudice she felt growing up poor and black on the lower East Side of Manhattan. Biographers, citing her rural Maine upbringing, believe these entries show the onset of her depression and a gradual descent into the delusional world that provoked the still-controversial "incident" two years later aboard the SS *Sunstruck*, when the ship foundered in shark-infested waters off the coast of Mexico.

[22] She seems to be intimating a plan to kill herself here, though details are carefully coded.

[23] "No flowers today from housekeeping" is thought to be a reference to her celibacy. A journal entry from the same time: "S. is COOL to me now. She locks herself in her room at the hotel and PRETENDS NOT TO BE AT HOME. But I can HEAR HER IN THEIR [sic] WALKING!" (Scholars note the strange grammatical error, the first of a series of uncharacteristic mistakes that would eventually overwhelm her writing and destroy her communicative abilities.)

[24] Even as events in the "real world" became increasingly troubling for the author, she continued to wax theoretical about the disconnect between language and world: "It is not," she claimed in "Philosophical Assay #85," "S.'s lack of affection for me that causes me such pain, but the language by which

I mediate that effect." Again, in "#87," she states, "Pain is a linguistic phenomenon. I feel "pain" in large part because I have a word for it."

[25] In this section, the author's abilities with language are eroding, yet most commentators feel that this is the most powerful passage in the entire opus. Harold Broom of Manchester University has written in *Witness to an Execution: Last Poems of Madeleine du Plessix* that du Plessix's "gradual disintegration" is an emblem for "the artist's unquenchable thirst for both language and reality, a doubling that results in a terminally divided self. The demands of du Plessix's two masters are incommensurate and result in the destruction of the author herself. This is the pure language of pain—unintelligible, senseless, and despite itself, ruthlessly delightful."

[26] The several references to Prospero in this final section are most often taken as codified foreshadowings of the author's undoing.

[27] Here du Plessix echoes Paul de Man's famous statement that "death is a displaced name for a linguistic predicament." Perhaps a more appropriate quotation, found in one of her unsent letters to S., comes from Michel Foucault: "... death is power's limit, the moment that escapes it."

[28] "Sea, rise up and mete [*meet?*]. Torn water's mouth. / Heavy with paine, I sink. Sank." The measure is vague, the writing dissolute, but the meaning is clear and ominous. The bilingual pun on "Sank (*Cinque*)" remains a chilling final note: Madeleine

du Plessix apparently cast herself into the Gulf of Mexico's shark-infested waters from the tailfin of the SS *Sunstruck* on September 5.

Charles Cutler, Dan Mahoney & Gaby Gordon-Fox, eds.

To Mr. Poe, from His Beautiful Annabel Lee

My dear Mr. Poe, you silly twit, to sleep so by the sea!
I'm dead, you're not, and that is why it's over between you and me.
Get a house in town, get a job, clear your head;
Get dressed, comb your hair, find a girl who's not dead
    Like your beautiful Annabel Lee.

We loved, it is true, and we walked by the sea.
We walked and we walked and we walked, didn't we?
Angels didn't much envy our romance, my twitness,
They envied the cardiovascular fitness
    Of your beautiful Annabel Lee.

Ed, I hated that beach, the sand and the sun
(The moon by the time you and I were quite done
Walking that beach in the rain in the wind).
Bedraggled, I'd wallow; you'd breathe deep and grin,
    "You're beautiful, Annabel Lee."

Oh, it's true we were children; we walked by the sea.
It's true, I loved you, and I guess you loved me.
True, you pointed to stars, to the moon, to the tides.
Still, I wish you'd had *something* to tell me besides
    "You're beautiful, Annabel Lee."

But now that I'm dead, you're walking no more.
You're balding, you're fat, and you've started to snore.
I look down from this heaven, and I must confide
I'm glad I have left what you're sleeping beside—
    The body of Annabel Lee.

Are you happier now that I've not much to say?
I'm consistently pretty–don't have a bad day.
It's your favorite dress and my hair is arranged—
Come to think of it, Eddie, not too much has changed
    For beautiful Annabel Lee.

And I'm so glad to know our souls won't be "dissevered,"
While you sleep with my body—you're ever so clever.
Poor Annabel Lee, you've bedazzled, bedeviled her.
But I guess I was always just a roll in the sepulchre.
    Signed, beautiful Annabel Lee.

Mark DeCarteret

Slip

I manage less and less of myself here
and what I manage is less and less sound.
Were you able to make out that last sentence
with my mind wired shut and these hyphens-for-being?
No, I'm not by the sea here, never have been
but the sea's never far from those thoughts
of myself as a boy as he thought of the sea
and how the world had no words for it
and how now I have no words for the world.
So, from the start, they've been onto me
and what I've been at as I was writing this:
seeing if the page gets it righted this once.
But it's the usual froth and mouthed benedictions,
more empty dreams I've provoked into haloes.
I'll forever be haunted by what little comes after me,
those words I whiteout but can never think to leave.

Sharon Dolin

Ode to Fernando Pessoa
from Álvaro de Campos

Ah, dolorous lucid grand limpid electrical fabricator.
Tensile-fevered scribbler.
Scribble, arranging our identities to part with distant bells
For a distant bell, totally concealed, antagonizes.

Who wrote us, who engineers us, grrrrowwwl eternal!
Oh for trespassing retinal mechanisms in fury!
I'm fury far out and within,
For all my selves—nervous desiccated forest,
For all of us—pupils for a day to come to quays where you sit!
Take hold of us with dry lips or grand rude modern horns.

You gave us our beard amazingly of pearl,
Gave expression to all of us minus sensation,
Like excessive contemporaneous divas or maquettes.

I'm feverish in hand—motorized like tropical Nature—
Randy as tropical humans—day ferry and fog and forcible—
Can't do, can do presently, bang tambourine or
Past be our future,
Pork or pheasant, his is to add or peasant.

He has platonic and virginal entrails deluding us electrical.
Soporific aurora, he's a human forum, a Virgil and Plato,
He peddles to Alexander the Great, to a secular Talmud sins
    quaintly.

Charles Cutler, Dan Mahoney & Gaby Gordon-Fox, eds.

Adam's cave of tears,
Cerebral escalator to secular seeming,
A damper ecstasy curries transmission for these symbols are
    volunteers,
Rouging, raging, cheering, struggling, ferrying,
Fashion me an excess of caresses oh numinous corporeal
    caress of elms.

Ah, power, express me like a motor-sex in prime!
Complete me like mama can, ah!
Pose derriere (not vital), triumphant like a late-model car!
Pose me not penetrate me physically of all you are,
Raise, guard me to do ... ah, briar me completely.
Doses of perfume, or layered or lured and carved
Destined to floral stupendous, black, artificial and insatiable!

Alas, ruin us, alas break us, hell ho *la foule!*
To do or keep as "to do or keep jasmine mountains!"
Commerce; invaders; crooks exaggeratedly well-dressed;
Members evidently of aristocratic clubs;
Squalid figures too biased; family chefs vaguely for lease
And paternity not current, hearing it traversed. Oh
Call it day algebra ... ah algebra!
All passes, all that passes and never passes!
Presence emaciated accentuated does cook us!
Banality interesting (and can a sage keep her indentured?)
Dazed bourgeois, may he fill her generously,
A feminine grace is false to those pederasts that pass lean-tos;
And today the simplest of gents elegantly

Capers and sequesters himself.
He finally tunes-almost-your labyrinth.
Ah, come, you desire sere or satin, near-distant total.

Oh fashion us mountains! Oh mannequins! Oh ultimate
    figurines!
Oh arty girls in utero cater to a gent that can compare!
Oh the grand Amazons come vying sexually!
Oh the electric announcers gave him a stare and he disappeared!
Oh lactating comes like a blue-jay, construes he is different.
Hey, cemetery, our mother, cement baton, new voice processors!
Progress equals armaments gloriously mortified!
Cure us, as canoes, metal-haters, submariners, airplanes!

Ah, move us totally, attitude: calm an affair.
Ah move us carnivorously,
Minor voice and vista, or coitus grande, banal, you tease
Oh coitus totally modern
Oh minors contemporaneous, form—actual and proximate—
Does his system immediately calm the Universe!
Now revel, a cow metallic, dynamic, deistic!

Up the whole jokeway, haste to the Derby,
Murder enters dentists until you capture dust! (Chorus:
A certain alto could enter through nonhuman portals!
and the old harem mimes:
"Alas, alas, alas, cat and dry!
Geisha me, porter a cab, inside encounter us, voices, sequin us."

"Hey, Sir Levantine," "do da rude chicken of blood.")
Seems no one savors them a sou!

Oh feral waves, oh aluminum old champions of feral ululators!
Oh keys, oh ports, oh come boys, oh "gwan in da states," "oh revoke all doors!"

Oh moment truncated like a foggy road,
Oh moment of striding rude men, noisy and mechanical,
Oh moment dynamical passing him to dance as bacchantes.
So fair and so bronze baby dares a dosie-do with eyes.

No one says "I exist au-pair." Jeered, derided, engender me.
Encat me in all our combinations.
Eye me in all our skies.
Gee, our general does helixes with all our natives.

Gull, gar, like all porcelain similitudes! Hoopla!
Ah, no. Sere us today apart!
Oh no sir. You today are a gent and today's a party!

Homophonic translation based on Pessoa's "Triumphal Ode."

Amy Dryansky

Untitled

"I'm looking to the future," she said, removing the cerise pouch from beneath her sawdust hat, its stitched-on seed pearls glittering in the dark armory basement. "I won't volunteer that information, not to you or any other would-be rescuer; this is not a boat and I'm no sea shell, see?" We had stopped at the Bay of Fundy and the stink of it made me want to throw the doors open and inflate my emergency raft. The air was thick and woolen, the hotel dark. Ahead of us a stratified field, a layer cake of shell, rock, sand, weeds, but the sea itself ignored our drama: languorous, it spit spray half-heartedly while cuttlefish raced pipers along the water line. "You are not my rescuer," she said again, and it felt true. I had no suture for this kind of hurt, no rusty entreaty to offer that might skewer her loneliness, catch her up, however briefly, on my template.

Charles Cutler, Dan Mahoney & Gaby Gordon-Fox, eds.

STEPHEN DUNN

At the Restaurant

> *Life would be unbearable if we made ourselves conscious of it*
> —Pessoa

Six people are too many people
and a public place the wrong place
for what you're thinking—

stop this now.

Who do you think you are?
The duck à l'orange is spectacular,
the flan the best in town.

But there among your friends
is the unspoken, as ever,
chatter and gaiety its familiar song.

And there's your chronic emptiness
spiraling upward in search of words
you'll dare not say

without irony.
You should have stayed at home.
It's part of the social contract

In the Footsteps of a Shadow

to seem to be where your body is,
and you've been elsewhere like this,
for Christ's sake, countless times;

behave, feign.

Certainly you believe a part of decency
is to overlook, to let pass?
Praise the Caesar salad. Praise Susan's

black dress, Paul's promotion and raise.
Inexcusable, the slaughter in this world.
Insufficient, the merely decent man.

Charles Cutler, Dan Mahoney & Gaby Gordon-Fox, eds.

J. Paul Dutterer

The Gray Fables of Aesop S: July 29th

Today I lost part of my body.

Maybe a molar is too humble to even mention, but I know better. Many of my acquaintances, well a few of them, have had whole litanies of injuries. No doubt some of them see me and think, "He's too tired, but otherwise he's unfailingly healthy." And then they offer up a curse in the form of a smile. What do they know?

One of the countless dentists I consulted told me, "You have an abscess. Think of it as a poisonous subterranean river, sapping your strength. And then one day …" Well, I didn't need to be persuaded. I let only a single year elapse before making an appointment. Now this was the hour, so off to the small, dim office tucked away in a building that was bulging with the sheer number of dreary businesses holed up there.

Soon enough, I was in *the chair*: that place where everyone is a child. The dentist was quite smitten with his new assistant, apparently so new that she didn't know where any of the tools were. She wore silver eyeliner, which had a hypnotic effect. Despite the distraction she provided, he quickly and capably removed the embattled molar with the help of some oversized forceps. I intended to ask if I could see it before they disposed of it, but too much was going on. My tooth is like some sickly little brother who has been dragged off to the orphanage. The wound was closed with sutures; long strands of thread entered and re-entered my mouth. Immediately afterward, this maestro ran off to some other operation. Amber, as the assistant may have been called, stayed behind to explain various follow-up procedures. Rules for eating, gargling, and taking medicine were quickly relayed to me. As I got up, Amber seemingly tried to pat me on the shoulder. Her fingers barely touched me. Already, all things were starting to feel muffled, not only numb but even quiet.

It will be a few days until solid food is on my plate. But I will not be the same. Part of me that has been there since childhood is absent. Above the gap, another molar has lost its mastication partner. Whenever I eat, the lonely upper tooth will swing down and, to its continuing surprise, encounter a void.

Charles Cutler, Dan Mahoney & Gaby Gordon-Fox, eds.

Erica Ehrenberg

Pessoa Is Willing

Pessoa is willing to sit at the desk just shy
of the leak from the hole in the ceiling
even though it has been raining for days.
The circumference of the hole admits a high-
pitched light, white and opaque,
so that all shadows in the black lining
of his jacket are eradicated, all folds
now bear no weight
and if he closes his eyes he is the lone
passerby at the banks of a tiny river.
Through its wellspring he would be able to fit
only the top of his head. The bodies formed
in the streams of the water speak to him.
He arranges in the new light the files of the archive
to which he has been for some years now unwaveringly
dedicated. Hands born in the pressure
of the water come to rest on his shoulders
and his face. They are soft
as humidity itself, but reach with the impatience
of women at the water pump or in the fields.

Lynn Emanuel

Walt, I Salute You!
after Pessoa

From the Year Of Our Lord 20**,
from the Continent of the Amnesias,
from the back streets of Pittsburgh
from the little lit window in the attic
of my mind where I sit brooding and smoking
like a hot iron, Walt, I salute you!
Here we are. In Love! In a Poem!
Slouching toward rebirth in our hats and curls!
Walt, I'm just a woman, chaperoned, actual, vague and hysterical!
Outwardly, my life is one of irreproachable tedium,
inside, like you, I am in my hydroelectric mode.
The infinite and abstract current of my description
launches itself at the weakling grass. Walt, everything I see I am!
Nothing is too small for my interest in it!
I am undone in the multiplication
of my perceptions. Mine is a life alive with the radioactivity
of its former lives!
I am in every dog and hairpin! They are me! I am you!
All is connected in the great seethe of seeing and being,
the great oceans and beaches of speeding and knowing.
I groan and surge, I long for hatches and engine sumps
for sailors in undershirts and big pectorals.
Walt! You have me by the throat! Everywhere I turn you rise up
      insurmountable and near.
You have already been every Conestoga headed to California
that broke down in a cul-de-sac of cannibalism in the Rockies!

You have been every sprouting metropolis re-routed
through three generations of industrialists!
You, the sweat of their workers' brows! You, their hatred of poets!
You have been women! Women with white legs, women with
    black mustaches,
waitresses with their hands glued to their rags on the counter,
waitresses in Dacron who light up the room with their serious
    wattage!
Yes! You are magically filling up, like milk in a glass, the white
nylon uniform, the blocky shoes with their slab of rubber sole!
Your hair is a platinum helmet! At your breast, a bouquet of
    Rayon violets!
And you have been places! You have been junkyards with their
    rusted Hoovers,
the pistils of wilted umbrellas.
And then, on the horizon (you have been the horizon!)
Walt, you are a whole small town erupting!
You are the drenched windows. The steaming gutters.
The streets black and slick as iron skillets.
The tawdry buildings. The rooms rented.
And now, in total hallucination and inhabitation, tired of being
    yourself—
Walt, the champ, the chump, the cheeky—you become me!
My every dark and slanderous thought. Walt, I salute you!
And therefore myself! In our enormous hats! In our huge
    mustaches!
We can't hide! We recognize ourselves!

Joshua Jennifer Espinoza

It Is Important to Be Something

This is like a life. This is lifelike.
I climb inside a mistake
and remake myself in the shape
of a better mistake—
a nice pair of glasses
without any lenses,
shoes that don't quite fit,
a chest that always hurts.
There is a checklist of things
you need to do to be a person.
I don't want to be a person
but there isn't a choice,
so I work my way down and
kiss the feet.
I work my way up and lick
the knee.
I give you my skull
to do with whatever you please.
You grow flowers from my head
and trim them too short.
I paint my nails nice and pretty
and who cares. Who gives a shit.
I'm trying not to give a shit
but it doesn't fit well on me.
I wear my clothes. I wear my body.
I walk out in the grass and turn red
at the sight of everything.

Charles Cutler, Dan Mahoney & Gaby Gordon-Fox, eds.

Sandy Feinstein

Pen Names

The lookout is you
in those castles *sans* kings
a one-man poetical crew
aloft on multiple wings.

St. Jorge on the hill
of Visigoths and Moors
picturesque as a quill,
the matter of metaphors
that make up your faces,

Stare of the sea's
conquering races

All in Portuguese.

Mary Dingee Fillmore

Love Stories

It could almost be you, a boy
driving us into the dark,
and it could surely be me, a drowsy teenager
forty years ago, my hand on your thigh
until you found somewhere dark
enough, still but for cicadas calling,
calling, like my hand
taking yours from the wheel,
my mouth finding the cavern
of yours. You grew under my hand,
a marvel like spring
speeded up. When did I first know
the flood of you, the millions
in my hand flailing their minute tails,
sudden and sloppy, fragrant as birth?
When did I learn rapture
from the body I'd maintained with disdain
like a half dead jalopy?

It could almost be you
as you return to me in dreams,
past the static between us,
the betrayals, the lengthy diminuendo.
In the night you are again only kind,
only reaching into the dark,
your hands skimming my skin
like dragonflies on a shuddering pool,

then our bodies indistinguishable from one another,
no withdrawals, and no barriers.

It could almost be you driving
us, and it could almost be me—
but instead the thigh is fuller,
a woman's limb, and my fingers
aren't electric with the new
but soak like fine rain into
a well traveled path.
Her face, lit by a passing car,
turns slightly, the lopsided
beginning of a smile that knows
where this is headed. It's not
the dream: we have to wrangle
with sniffles and underwear
whose elastic is going, the lash
of irritation over milk gone sour,
a door left unlocked, a crack to repair.
Still, in French train berths, cheap
or costly hotels by seasides
or peaks, in our own varied beds,
she and I have found our way
within: the caverns slippery
with longing, the spiraling muscles strong
to push a baby out, arms holding
what was never held before—all
this, for more years
than you and I had even lived

In the Footsteps of a Shadow

when we rode in that other
car. The road's the same,
but this time it's headed to a bed
made again and again.

Charles Cutler, Dan Mahoney & Gaby Gordon-Fox, eds.

Deborah Finkelstein

Things

> *How could a man who was so fond of things*
> *Never have looked at them or understood what they were?*
> —Alberto Caeiro

The fire is simply the fire.
It is not inspiration or passion.
It is not dancing souls making love.
Or the devil singing on the dirt.
It warms the water,
heats my chilled fingers
and cooks my food.

The sun is simply the sun.
It is not a gift from the Gods.
It is not Apollo or Helios or Ra.
It is not power or justice.
It warms my home,
and draws my salad
from the ground.

The rain is simply the rain.
It is not tears.
It is not the place for sad lovers.
Or the place to be cleansed.
It brings me drink,
feeds the flowers
and cleans my walk.

These things do not make life good.
These things do not make life bad.
These things are what make life life.

Charles Cutler, Dan Mahoney & Gaby Gordon-Fox, eds.

Frank Gaspar

I Am Not a Keeper of Sheep

How little I knew about the world when I let him in,
even though now I can't remember the day or time,
I can't remember what random thought guided my
hand in such an innocent act. I say this because it is
of no importance whatsoever on a hot August night,
a drink by my elbow, the cat speaking his mad language
against the window screens, and the blossoms of
so many papers and books in a desultory mess in the little
room. I have been reading without decorum or discipline—
the shelves are manic, nothing takes its civil place
according to alphabet or color or size. The center
cannot hold because it was never there in the first place.
One must never let Pessoa across the threshold. I can say
this with a sober mind for just a while longer. He sits
so unassumingly at the table and you give him a small
drink, and he begins to speak to you, and then you realize
your day is ruined, your plans will come to nothing, you
will end by trying every subterfuge you know to get him
to leave, but he will wait and wait. And he is so charming!
He will tell you stories, and you will recognize yourself in every
sentence—you will understand quite quickly that he is mocking
you, but then you will begin to doubt that, for he is so sincere,
so simple in his utterance, so passionate in his beliefs. How
can you not offer him another *cafezinho*, which I do, which
he sips noisily but with a certain finesse. Then I begin feeling
sorry for myself—that old sorrow—and I wish that someone
a long time ago cared for me enough to warn me, to tell me never

to let Pessoa into my kitchen, never to let him go on and on about *his* sadness, that sadness that never leaves him no matter how happy or content he feels, for then there is no hope for him and none for me, and he at least has his genius to sit with, his personalities, his Lisbon, his Tagus, and I, like you, will have to settle for his company, wry, effacing, enigmatic, too delicate for hearty jesting, too prickly and gloomy to be of any real use around the house. Then the hours do not grow late in the same manner. The rooms do not simmer and cool in quite the way that I have become used to. The doors are no longer silent on their hinges. The planks in the floor begin their own conversations. So many things become impossible. He drags a match across the abrasive strip of the matchbox. The phosphorus makes its shushing sound. He lights another cigarette. His fingers are so white, so slender, his wrist is like a girl's wrist. *I am not a keeper of sheep,* he says. The night will be long and soft with stars and the heat and the ticking of one heart or another. He leans back in the chair with that uncertain charisma, that narrow head. I can tell he is here to stay.

Charles Cutler, Dan Mahoney & Gaby Gordon-Fox, eds.

A Witness Gives His Version

I am someone other than an "I" of whom I do not know if he exists ...
    —Fernando Pessoa

    I don't know how I know this,
but if simple presence could hover
in a room unseen, then I was
the one who watched that tenderest
labor as the woman, her head bound
in a white kerchief, silently bent
over the corpse, washing it with
a fistful of cloth that she dipped
into an enameled basin and wrung
dripping with both raw hands.
Others were in that room. I saw them.
Some were neighbors, clearly come
to proffer aid and experience.
One man lingered, dressed in gray
wool pants that hung from leather braces.
He looked dazed and immeasurably sad
as only a man could look who would not
be permitted to weep in his station
as man in this tiny house of rough boards.
Against the back wall, by the doorway
to another room, stood the iron stove,
and upon it the copper utensils. I
was nowhere, I was nothing, for there was

no I yet to bear witness, and still
I was present when they wrapped the body
in the winding cloth, swaddling the limbs
        and tying the jaw

      It's enough, you might say, for me
to tell you this—the way someone
might speak of a dream over coffee,
dreamily pensive, touching on some
useful meaning as though every tale
were allegory and bore upon a life.
But these other lives—*their* lives—
they could never have known me among them.
Would we say they are merely vocabulary,
this gaunt dead woman and her ministers?
It might do, for the other explanations
are tedious, and yet I might go farther
and tell you that I remember another
door behind me, and that I knew what
lay beyond it, the dark, pre-electric
village street, the gray ocean water,
never far, the other board houses,
the picket fences, the winter-dead roses
on the fine trellises: and suddenly
because there was no *I*, I became
the angel or the ghost, and I was moved
by their sorrow and their mortal plight.
And because they might have sensed me
there or thought, even fleetingly, that

they were not alone, I fled until I came
to this convenient place of forgetting,
before they might have imputed something
untoward to me, wisdom or power
or the smallest ability to intervene.

Joseph Gastiger

Little Things That Get Lost

Socks, gloves, famously. Badges, insignia
first, I was proud to wear; and then, ashamed.
Scapular, rosary, filled with mysterious
power until, one summer evening,

they were gone. But it's not only tokens
that disappear. I miss the way I'd feel
sweating in the fields, gobbling an orange,
listening to opera on the radio.

Mainly, I miss how women looked at me
before I vanished, too, with my umbrella,
my fedora and, perhaps, gold cufflinks—
as indistinguishable as they come.

Charles Cutler, Dan Mahoney & Gaby Gordon-Fox, eds.

In a Certain Light

If I could, I'd squeeze all that I still want
to tell you into the time it takes
to smoke a cigarette after my coffee
after a fine, fine meal, leaving a small

ristorante one evening, early
September, perhaps in Trieste, as you
grab hold of my arm for a moment
whether by habit or accident, and

I realize this can't be happening—
I haven't smoked in years—though sometimes I
want to when I almost turn to see you
Lia, in a certain light.

San Marino

I should have been born in a country
too small to nurse any wilder ambition
than wanting to prepare a simple meal
for people I love. I would set jonquils

on the table, figs and pears, pour out
the wine I have been saving for a day
like this.   Later, after the veal,
rabbit, or *pici*, or whatever else,

we might sit quietly as we sip
Strega, watching the stars come out above
a castle no one's defended or tried
to capture for hundreds of years.

Charles Cutler, Dan Mahoney & Gaby Gordon-Fox, eds.

ALLEN GINSBERG

Salutations to Fernando Pessoa

Everytime I read Pessoa I think
I'm better than he is I do the same thing
more extravagantly—he's only from Portugal,
I'm American greatest Country in the world
right now End of xx Century tho Portugal
had a big empire in the 15th century never mind
now shrunk to a Corner of Iberian peninsula
whereas New York take New York for instance
tho Mexico City's bigger NY's richer think of Empire State
Building not long ago world empire's biggest skyscraper—
be that as't may I've experienced 61 years' XX Century
Pessoa walked down Rua do Ouro only till 1936
He entered Whitman so I enter Pessoa no
matter what they say besides dead he wouldn't object.

What way'm I better than Pessoa?
Known on 4 Continents I have 25 English books he only 3
his mostly Portuguese, but that's not his fault—
U.S.A.'s a bigger Country
merely 2 Trillion in debt a passing freakout,
Reagan's dirty work an American Century aberration
unrepresenting our Nation Whitman sang in Epic manner
tho worried about in Democratic Vistas
As a Buddhist not proud my superiority to Pessoa
I'm humble Pessoa was nuts big difference,
tho apparently gay—same as Socrates,
consider Michelangelo Da Vinci Shakespeare

inestimable comrado Walt
True I was tainted Pinko at an early age a mere trifle
Science itself destroys ozone layers this era antiStalinists
poison entire earth with radioactive anticommunism
Maybe I lied somewhat
rarely in verse, only protecting other's reputations
Frankly too Candid about my mother tho meant well
Did Pessoa mention his mother? she's interesting,
powerful to birth sextuplets
Alberto Caeiro Álvaro de Campos Ricardo Reis Bernardo Soares
   && Alexander Search simultaneously

with Fernando Pessoa himself a classic sexophrenic
Confusing personae not so popular
outside Portugal's tiny kingdom (till recently a second-rate police
   &state)
Let me get to the point er I forget what it was
but certainly enjoy making comparisons between this Ginsberg
   && Pessoa
people talk about in Iberia hardly any books in English
presently the world's major diplomatic language extended
   &throughout China.
Besides he was a shrimp, himself admits in interminable
   &"Salutations to Walt Whitman"

Whereas 5'70" height
somewhat above world average, no immodesty,
I'm speaking seriously about me & Pessoa.
Anyway he never influenced me, never read Pessoa

before I wrote my celebrated "Howl" already translated into
    24 languages,
not to this day's Pessoa influence an anxiety
Midnight April 12–88 merely glancing his book
certainly influences me in passing, only reasonable
but reading a page in translation hardly proves "Influence."
Turning to Pessoa, what'd he write about? Whitman,
(Lisbon, the sea etc.) method peculiarly longwinded,
diarrhoea mouth some people say—Pessoa Schmessoa.

Laura Glenn

Faking It

> The poet is a faker
> Who's so good at his act
> He even fakes the pain
> Of pain he feels in fact.
> —Fernando Pessoa

If you feel dismal,
sometimes it's better
to act
the way you feel

when you're hopeful,
like the inverse of Pessoa,
who "fakes the pain … he feels"
in poetry. Take care

not to feel the pain you fake;
there's enough real pain
you can fake not feeling
in hope of convincing yourself.

And if the pain you fake is real …
Never mind.
Return to your canvas: a splotch of color,
like a small sun, escapes your brush.

Charles Cutler, Dan Mahoney & Gaby Gordon-Fox, eds.

Try to re-create the happiness
that radiates from the mistake—
though half the time
you botch the canvas up.

David B. Goldstein

Burning Doll

Bernardo Soares returned from work
down the street of goldsmiths.
When I raise my hands, it rains.
When I dodge leaves, it burns.

Lenita Gentil took me up to the balcony
to procure me a husband.
She told me one may clean a fish
with dull scissors and a mallet.

The dog hoarses himself by barking.
The hill wearies itself by climbing.
You hear me as I am, little mad one,
for I am ready to paint your portrait.

Charles Cutler, Dan Mahoney & Gaby Gordon-Fox, eds.

Anne Gorrick

Jerry Freedman Thinks He's Fernando Pessoa

Jerry Freedman thinks he's Fernando Pessoa
an angular architecture in front of his Nikon.
His glasses, goatee and junk store stoic

porkpie arranged to house several voices blowing,
in a perfect universe, across photographic film. An icon
in four fragments, Jerry Freedman thinks he's Fernando Pessoa.

The portraits unexpectedly rowing
across black into white, toward a visually rhyming land:
    Saigon, freon, Gloire de Dijon
behind his glasses, goatee and junk store stoic

His face divides into quadrants not unlike Rimbaud
at his best, the division occurring at a cellular level, neon
grids splitting the interior color field while Jerry Freedman
    thinks he's Fernando Pessoa

The actual photos seem dipped in Corot
and washed in the feathers of starlings. Even though his suit is
    rayon and cheap,
Jerry Freedman still thinks he's Fernando Pessoa

He will attempt to capture the intellectual Latin gardens sown
    in the regenerative ionic

process called "photography." Jerry Freedman's tropism is
   toward Fernando Pessoa
seen through his glasses, goatee and junk store, stoic

Charles Cutler, Dan Mahoney & Gaby Gordon-Fox, eds.

ROBERT GRAY

A Selected Pose of Fernando Pessoa

Consider his wretched love
letters to Ophelia Queiroz,
a postal affair sabotaged
by Álvaro de Campos;
the ventriloquist's seduction
unraveled by his dummy's
slivered tongue.

A doomed course
mapped in salutations:

Ophelia, My dear darling baby,
Dear naughty little baby,
Little baby,
Dear Ophelia,
Dear Miss Ophelia Queiroz,
Terrible baby,
Beastly baby.

As Pessoa's readers, his collaborators,
were amused by, even used to,
his straightjacket obsession,
formal wear complement
to stripped self-awareness:

I realize that all this is comical, and
that the most comical part of it is me.

Gradually we witness
the pathos of descent.
Álvaro discreetly undermines:

*As the sincere and close friend
of the good-for-nothing
whose message I have (reluctantly)
undertaken to communicate ...*

We laugh with Pessoa
because he is brilliant.
Were he less brilliant,
we might laugh at him.

If Pessoa wasn't Pessoa,
we couldn't bear to read him.

Charles Cutler, Dan Mahoney & Gaby Gordon-Fox, eds.

Timothy Green

American Fractal

We are like two chasms,
a well staring up at the sky
—Fernando Pessoa, *The Book of Disquiet*

two mirrors face each other   my hands over my face   the

porcelain soap dish   an angel's wings & a mile of its offerings

pink on pink on black tile   I'm in the bathroom   close the door

shut the light   down the hall the tv too loud   bob barker & *the*

price is right   shut that out too   I'm on the other edge of

something   of adulthood   of a gulf   a canyon   looking

down down   no vultures circling picking bones though   no

heaped bodies to climb over   no fall to cushion   or to be

cushioned   not the body that matures this time   just this

hollow wooden door   the lock my parents could pick with a belt-

hook at any moment   the hot glare of the vanity lights   making

In the Footsteps of a Shadow

my pimples glow   I said shut the light   shut the light   the tv

too loud mother won't get up   get up!   the friend visiting

from florida   her baby james sucking grapes   he wouldn't eat

anything else   just the grapes   the seedless orbs like eyeballs

sucking them   each green globe with a little pop   a little giggle

wouldn't take the formula   wouldn't take the mashed carrots &

peas   brown mush from a jar   the rubber spoon an airplane

but still nothing   a silent protest maybe maybe reading into

things too far   we fed him grapes for three weeks   he kept

giggling   sleeping in my bedroom   a crib of blankets in

the cedar hope chest at the foot of my bed grapes & grapes & the

husband flying up finally to take him home   to take her home

a quiet man   a mustache   all five-foot-five of him fumbling

down the hall the showcase showdown   the systolic bleep of the wheel slowing to rest   a dinette set   a new car   flashing

lights   cheers & screams from the audience   mother's best

friend in the intersection held her baby   cat-walked the dotted

yellow line & then sat down   the baby crying   the headlights

horns   she sat down   then the police call at midnight. do you

know the father?   then driving home holding the baby while my

father shifted & swore   the soft skull   the soft neck   way

past bedtime   past due   stay up! stay up! his head so

heavy   mother on the couch again won't get up   won't blink

a crack in the ceiling holding her there   mesmerized   like the

root of that word something animal   doctoral   doctor mesmer

on his glass armonica   the women in tubs of glass powder

iron fillings   the magic of the wand   relax relax   my sweet

baby james   singing from behind the curtain   go to sleep. go

In the Footsteps of a Shadow

to sleep   they had words for it back then   hysteria

distemper   the doctors in the waiting room more mysterious

more clinical   we had clinics now   post-partum depression

they said   bipolar disorder   they said in their white robes

behind their stethoscopes & clipboards   their shoes so soft they

moved soundlessly down the long hall   the price is right on a

television hanging from the ceiling   I sit down in the bathtub

how can you blame them for sitting down   things getting so

heavy?   for what do we hold onto eventually?   m Eventually

what don't we hold onto?   mother in the living room.   on the

couch   shake her shake her   wake her up. & father   at the

bar he says   ate at work he says   & the bathroom with its

cheap lock   that convenient clasp   & the light on   & the

light off & the mirror into mirror into mirror   that silver-backed glass   looking like her   looking like him.   the images

playing off   themselves in the glass   divide   divide & how

could they know   each one   each image into infinity   how

could they know?   each image one moment behind the last

catching up & catching up   until the last   & finally letting go

the last   like a leap into no faith   letting go   that smallest star

that grain of sand   that simplest & finest point of light

Joan Haladay

Trilha Pessoa

Fernando Pessoa:
you follow me around
As a travel journal mention,
mistaken by Manoel for João,
you turned into place poem—
a northeast Brazilian town—
and fitting byway
to accompany my mouthing *Mensagem*
with Caetano, Elba, Gil
At Gas Station, a glacial place
where folks without stove heat
settled for dog flesh or breath
your poems blew sparks
You turned up in books:
Tabucchi's obsessed *Requiem*
and Saramago's *romance* of returns
In Lisboa, Maria and I
contemplated your Martinho da Arcada table shrine
consumed Brasileira coffee near your pigeon-perch statue
and performed a pilgrimage to Casa Pessoa
Riba de Castro caught me there too—
hatted—suitable for a momentary flight of Ophélia—
he settled at my table
in your trademark spectacles and a slippery moustache
oozing preoccupation and paper
Post-*almoço*, in the Prazeres
I found it already existed within his book:

Charles Cutler, Dan Mahoney & Gaby Gordon-Fox, eds.

place within place
Fernando Pessoa
peregrinating poet of the *praças*
your plaques are everywhere
Lisboa is Pessoa polis
poet of Place within place
poet of voices
poet of *pátria*
poet of poets
you follow me around

DANIEL HALES

How to Converse with a Stranger
for Álvaro de Campos

When I was a kid the Operator was one woman   omniscient
schoolmarm able to knit while plugging through every call in
the world   But now out the window   every sign's *Corporate
Interiors* or *Discount Sleep*   marquees warning this movie is
Rated X for Sadness   because even the most divine dreams
the kind I play and rewind for weeks were manufactured by
starving children in a Third World sweat-shop

I can't sleep on trains   Past sealed sills the outside world
drifts through its own dream   in which I'm required to
remain a small but alert part   nativity play shepherd who just
has to bow and stare adoringly at the miracle

A dream I do remember   I'm at the door counting my
machine's red winks   Instead of messages   though
recorded dreams the apartment had while I was out   In one
I get caught   turn myself in escape under assumed name
But they keep following and each place needs a new me

Soon unused heteronyms stalk me too   Bowling with
colleagues   an almost steady girl   when I'm invaded by Ulrich
Flint   Professor Vhümpeltaáz   Juan Doe   Luckily the
bathroom window slid open quietly and I only sprained an ankle
Stay a few limps ahead of scorned aliases   quick catch up with
your prettiest alibis don't fall in love with anyone or thing you're
likely to lose someday

Charles Cutler, Dan Mahoney & Gaby Gordon-Fox, eds.

Once I step off into my new town   I'll hold out this face like it's mine Maybe you'll be standing on the platform   will gesture for me to come share your umbrella   We could stand quietly together   listen to the rain   and as long as no one speaks   we can postpone our acquaintance   possible engagement   our inevitable parting

James Hannaham

Seeing and Thinking

What separates seeing and thinking? Anything? I have met people who liked their thoughts so much that they told me their thoughts about me as soon as they saw me. When they saw what they thought they saw when they saw me, an upside-down bogeyman flashed on their meatscreens, and the camera obscuras in their rapid eyes turned vitreous humor to tragic theater. They said a stupid wrong thing to me that they thought not just true, but clever and true. So they must be the same thing, the light and the thought, the thought and the light.

"The Keeper of Sheep (5)," Alberto Caeiro

Felt

We feel we have felt felt. We have felt what felt we have. Have felt. Feel. We feel what felt we felt is not what felt felt is. What we have, we feel. What felt we have! Feel! Feel not what is, feel what felt is not. Not we, not felt. Is is is? We is what we is, we felt what we feel not. Have not what is feel. Not is we is what we have feel. We not we is what felt not not feel have is not. Have we what what is what. Felt is what not feel we we what. Feel is felt we what not have is what feel felt felt we. Not what feel feel is felt have have have we is have felt is what have what.

"What we feel, not what is felt," Ricardo Reis

The Person in Question

A self consists primarily of unremembered events. The highest number of memories forgotten about a particular person will disappear from the mind of that same person. Usually this happens involuntarily, but some people suppress certain memories. Occurrences tangential to the person tend to retain even less staying power. Many of the moments relating to the person, when recalled, may also be misremembered. What few events anyone remembers may then be interpreted or twisted in any fashion by anyone who has ever had any contact with the subject, however indirect, as well as by those who have had no direct contact, or no contact of any kind. Interpretations of these events will then change, sometimes quite rapidly, based on the context in which they appear. False experiences may attach themselves to misremembered occurrences. The self can only keep a handful of its adventures in mind, and then explain itself to itself in wildly fluctuating ways until it becomes completely baffled by the nature of the human being at the center of its own story.

"Slanting Rain," Fernando Pessoa

Charles Cutler, Dan Mahoney & Gaby Gordon-Fox, eds.

The Death of the Critic

The editors worked meticulously, posthumously, to create a person.
In this process, they found, most joyously, job security for Michel Foucault.
In life, the person had worked to avoid personhood, despite his family name: Person.
If the world teaches you anything, it is that interpretation beats creation.
Wipe the language off everything and what do you have left? Some other planet.
The critics determined what constituted the work. They had the proper training.
They found the most egotistical occupations and planted their flag.
"An artist makes things, but exists less and less."
You are just a vehicle for the invention of a thing that I legitimize by deciphering it.
It figures you are a Gemini, Fernando.
The long-dead man had no recourse; he was a recorpse.

"I divide what I know," Fernando Pessoa

Myronn Hardy

Pessoa As Starling: New York City

Everything up   climbing up granite   steel.
A poet cries chrysanthemums. A vase
breaks in Harlem on Lenox before meals
are served to nuns   opal beads quick as lace
through conical fingers. A black feather falls
in black hair. His father has black hair sunned
brown in groves where I flew. Poems in groves walled
in loose stones but the poet needed the gun.
The father to send his sighing son to
the city's sighing streets where black women
saunter   sing   carry vases of water
sometimes salty   sometimes fresh. This given
to the poet unconsciously conscious
of riots   the street   the body conscious.

Charles Cutler, Dan Mahoney & Gaby Gordon-Fox, eds.

Pessoa As Starling: Lisbon

My father is dead as is my brother.
Absence is invisibility but
I feel   feel them in currents folding through
feathershills where cathedrals collide with
unconsciousness. Starshine glares with such whiteness
like crests. I dive into the hard crests of
this land like the Atlantic   salty with
subjugation. Not a bird of prey but
preyed upon. My silence   so insincere.
I tell you of this place   transcribe it through
another name   a man I make up   sing
to perhaps in a dream   through possession.
Call me mysterious. Alone   without
flock   I claim no one but they will claim me.

Pessoa As Starling: Tunis

That hollow building built in 1923
is a cage with windows
wide as wild. I fly over
Avenue Habib Bourguiba   perch
in trees pruned to green squares wondering
when again   the raucousness   the fragility
belief anchors.
My song is silence but theirs is not.
The rhythm of subversion
after nothing   after everything
red dries to skin. Tanks ready
to blast   barbed wire in pythons   military
on guard all warning to never
rage   never ask   never human   never.

Pessoa As Starling: Johannesburg

Dark feathers stuffing the pillow.
The feathers of my dead brother   you
sleep there on his feathers sewed in muslin.
You were born when Brazil ended slavery.
When my great-grandfather watched a black
woman sob beneath a pale awning.
Mahatma Gandhi hated blacks   arrived
in Durban when your father died. You knew
this disabling place even though young.
Sleeping on black feathers   black
illusions during sleep   such serenity.
We are pitch in a chromatic sky shrinking.
I was the bird who sang to another.

Megan Harlan

Ambient City

I close my eyes on the glowing city.
Inside is gregarious sleep.
Inside a city shining on the hill.
Particulates of inner resources.
Particulates of hell-or-high-water.
Particulates of midnight traffic.
Inside a fibrous architecture,
alive with witness, windows
opening on windows, snatches
of hair, books, ringing, equal portions
building and air.
Inside zoos of food and spirits,
flickering poses, animalism
played like a symphony.
Inside a crowd's fraying
lacework, heaped on
certain streets for centuries.
Outside, partial views
of several running disasters.
Inside, a shared and generous premise.
Inside ambition, torn open at the gut.
Outside, a glow seen from space.
Inside, manic conversations
with multiple sources of light:
Denial's moon-faced signals,
the gonging of chemical sunsets,
neon's iridescent ash

Charles Cutler, Dan Mahoney & Gaby Gordon-Fox, eds.

like the dark side all grown up.
Inside inroads to myself.
Inside, a sleep within a source.

Painted Sky

I stopped inside a church
in midtown for a few minutes,
its prolific gifts
collected over centuries
for someone else.
I have a fixed idea of life.
It is, I often suspect, entirely wrong.
It is solid as a building,
indoors on a beautiful day.
In a painted sky are creatures
with wings but no souls,
though how can we tell.
The soul is not body or stone.
The soul is an emptiness,
maybe filled with something
we can't see, like time,
time buried alive.
Our bodies forgive it, helplessly.
This emptiness also resembles
doubt. This emptiness resembles
the soaring air inside the church—
the shape of time as beauty,
or doubt as passion—
but I am literal-minded,
a story spent in flight,
like the stained-glass windows
radiant with midtown.

Charles Cutler, Dan Mahoney & Gaby Gordon-Fox, eds.

JEANETTE HENDRICKS (AS EMMA WATKINS)

Dizes-me: tu és mais alguma coisa

Drink to Me Only Under Water
I don't see how
you can tell someone
you love them thousands of times
and then just disappear.

Jeanette Hendricks (as Claire Jacobson)

A espantosa realidade das coisas

The frightening reality of things
is that in one second
you lose all your days
and everything you know.
It's difficult to explain
why something like that makes me so happy
and fills me.
It's enough that I exist
for me to feel complete.
I have written enough poems
easily enough.
In each poem,
I tried to say something,
and all my poems are different,
because everything in nature has its own way of being
and its own thing to say.
Sometimes I feel I need
to pray
or feel I need to fail to see,
or that I need him to feel.
Now he makes me change color like a chameleon.
It's easier to like him
when he prays,
easier to like him
because he doesn't see,
easier to like him

Charles Cutler, Dan Mahoney & Gaby Gordon-Fox, eds.

because he's with me
without parentheses.

Tony Hoagland

The Question

> We are what is missing from the world
> —Fernando Pessoa

Some questions have no answer.
Raised, they hang there in the mind
like open mouths, full of something missing.
The great Portuguese poet, Pessoa,
said that the idea of happiness
is what makes men permanently sad.
The body, imagining the soul,
looks ugly to itself.
A man hears a word, and the world
becomes a place that he misunderstands.
So he climbs high into his life,
ashamed of all he doesn't know,
and refuses to come down.

If you could coax him out again,
You could tell him, say,
That anything can be explained.
The shape of apples, for example,
By their love of travel.
Or that the sky is blue because
It's an easy color on the eyes.

Even the dog, chasing its tail,
Has, temporarily, a center.

Even the bird, disappearing into his hole
Knows that the world goes on without it.
And Pessoa, that eminently healthy man,
That artist, wore a blue wool hat
Even on the hottest summer days.
Simply to toss at strangers in the street.
He liked to see them catch it,
And grow immediately less strange.

Walter Holland

After Pessoa

1. (Caeiro)

Metaphysics? What metaphysics occur along this roadside?
The dead raccoon is flattened now into a shell of bone

with skeins of blood-red fur. By day the Ridgeway Mall has steady
streams of traffic and near the exits, beds of flowers, nasturtium

mixed with petunias. Thinking is discomfort. I have no plans.
Buy a latte, sit by Walmart, inspect the sale at nearby Sears.

What is a mystery? Shopping carts returned each
day from the lot? My gaze is maybe for a mile

or more, looking north down Route 3 past the Pizza Hut.
Kudzu straddles the banks of the river. In summer,

laurel comes out in the woods. A curve in the road
marks the death of two teens, years ago driving while

intoxicated—fresh-cut daisies in a single vase, changed every
    Saturday
by the side of the highway—but what can you do about suffering?

They've gouged out the ravine and filled in the creek,
I used to walk there in the fifties. The orchards

are gone with their branching fruit, the mill water thick
with algae. Mass is no longer said in the high school.

I work for a nursery beside McDonalds, talk about
planting, shade and light, frequency of watering, lengths of
    season—

there is no whole to which this all belongs. When I drive at five
it's still light and the moon appears near the Bryar Bridge

and everything seems changed from when I was a boy
who couldn't make a decision.

2. (Reis)

I prefer to believe in the sanctity of life. I trust the clichés about
 fortune
and fame. There's little consolation in life. Talk-shows tell you
 this. Each choice

brings guilt. People carry on about Michael Jackson. They speak
 of ideal innocence.
Sleep with a boy! Reality is always more or less what we want
 it to be.

Days are brief. Injustice everywhere. Celebrities must obey the
 laws.
We only have a small mortgage on Love. Michael is a mess,
 though successful

and wealthy. We live in our narrow corner of Freedom. The
 mind is bordered
by the limits of TV. We see American life from a distance.
 There is nothing

it can easily tell you. I can't be exuberant, get worked up about
 everything.
Simplicity, these days, is a valuable lesson. Therapy. Yoga.
 Medication.

Charles Cutler, Dan Mahoney & Gaby Gordon-Fox, eds.

History ignores most of what we do. Love and Glory don't
    really matter.
Wealth and love cast long shadows. Michael can't acknowledge

his inner fears. We can't control the winds of destiny. His
    likeness is strange
and I want to tell him: Youth fades. You live in Never-Never-
    Land.

3. (Campos)

Like seeing a good movie, or dining out every night.
There is a pleasure in living so close to the city. We

park most weekends near the entry to the Lincoln
Tunnel and see most plays recommended in the Times.

I often go to MOMA. The 4th and 5th floors now figure
heavy in abstraction—Picasso to Pollock, the century in images.

Two years ago, I underwent bypass surgery. Recovery was quick,
a miracle of science. I can walk six miles everyday on

a treadmill. I like to meet a girlfriend for drinks in town.
(Married once before—like me, she's Reform). She and I

admire design and architecture. We've been to Bilboa and
Falling Water. It's hard not at my age to slow down.

Some days I feel restless watching the news. I'm a bit of a loner.
I go on cruises—last September to Turkey.

Love and sex? I have trouble with erections. I feel I have to put
my time to good use, but it's sad to see the aging Boomers—

you'd thought you'd conquer the world, then the world changes.
I often feel tired. I go to my doctor. He says try Viagra—it's
    clinically proven.

Paul Hoover

Lisbon Story

Be quiet—a shadow is singing.
A shadow on a yellow wall
is singing about time,
and a man like time
is leaning against a blue wall.
But it's a shadow singing
its heart out in the night.

Beyond this room in the world,
the sounds of the world are passing.
All lives, all cities, are full of sound.
A woman sings of them.
The river and her song
are cutting into the world.

A shadow is moving its mouth....
lyric to distraction, a lyric separation
of world and time, thought and mind.
Shadow on the wall—yellow—
where the blue man listens.

This house on the street, dark.
This slant street in the city, small as streets are small.
A sound of birds flying and a sound of paper.

In the Footsteps of a Shadow

A sound of sharpening knives, quick,
and dogs lifting their legs, thick,
and the girl who drops her doll.

The blue man listens to the world making itself—
a shoe making distance, click,
and snow barely surviving
on the ground it has chosen, gone.
A world as shadow is passing.

But in the yellow room,
a handsome woman is singing, ending,
and the room and its sounds are dark.

I Am the Size of What I See
—Fernando Pessoa

You hurry but you are late
to every party and dinner date,
so naturally they begin without you.
Like a pale leaf through the window,
you make your entrance secretly.
Now you can shine in the corner
as quietly as any leaf,
rarely speaking and then in puzzles;
in English when they are Spanish,
in cliff-edge when they are hanging.
They are the size of what they see,
swimming in their vocabularies
of desire and principal interest.

You're a bird too young to fly,
a map without its pink and salmon.
You're so late you arrive on time,
and later slip out unnoticed,
not even a smudge on your glass.
They never knew what passed them.

You walk to the absolute corner,
where the roof of the sky
meets the limit of the eye
and a breath lasts a lifetime.

Beautiful dreamer,
you're the size of what you see.
The sky is the size of the sky,
and the sun is just the sun.
But a tree is the size of the flame
you hold in your fingers.

What shirt to wear to eternity
and tomorrow to dinner?
And what size will it be?
You're asking while you can.
There are things you can't forget
like the life before this one.

Charles Cutler, Dan Mahoney & Gaby Gordon-Fox, eds.

CHARLIE HUENEMANN

Give Me Monotony!

Monotonizing existence, so that it won't be monotonous.
Making daily life anodyne, so that the littlest thing will amuse.
—Bernardo Soares, *The Book of Disquiet*, translated by Richard Zenith

Senhor Soares goes on to explain that in his job as assistant bookkeeper in the city of Lisbon, when he finds himself "between two ledger entries," he has visions of escaping, visiting the grand promenades of impossible parks, meeting resplendent kings, and traveling over non-existent landscapes. He doesn't mind his monotonous job, so long as he has the occasional moment to indulge in his daydreams. And the value for him in these daydreams is that they are *not* real. If they were real, they would not belong to him. They would belong to others as public resources, and not reside in his own private realm. And what is more, if they were real, then what would he have left to dream? Far better, he thinks, "to have Vasques my boss than the kings of my dreams." It's more than that he doesn't mind his monotonous job. On the contrary: the more monotonous his existence, the better his dreams.

This is, of course, mere escapism from the crappy life he's stuck with. His attempt to justify his monotonous existence by saying that it allows for better daydreams is as see-through as an 8-dollar verification program. He's just coating his own unremarkable existence in cheap veneer. Soares, one might judge, should have the courage to make his life *really* better, to find something worth doing, worth taking pride in, and something of some value to others. He should dare to live dangerously. Maybe he could start a book club. There's nothing wrong with daydreams, okay, but they should serve only as an occasion for a busy person to "recharge" and then return with greater focus to an active, productive life.

But as one gets older and realizes that most of life's good stuff is contained between two ledger entries, one sees that if it weren't for dreams, for stories and for art, for inventing personas and writing books through their hands and eyes, life would be insufferable. This is because our brains are too big. We are overpowered for the tasks modern life assigns us, and if we narrowed our focus to just what's actually before us, we would find ourselves on the road with Estragon and Vladimir, surveying a bleak Beckettian stage, haunted by a vague sense that wasn't there supposed to be something more, someone showing up who would make a difference?

Only a fictional keeper of sheep (with no sheep) like Alberto Caeiro (Fernando Pessoa, again) could possibly live with only the surfaces of things:

> To not think of anything is metaphysics enough
>
> To think about the *inner meaning of things*
> *Is superfluous, like thinking about health*
> *Or carrying a glass to a spring.*
> *The only inner meaning of things*
> *Is that they have no inner meaning* at all.
>
> Translated by Richard Zenith in *Fernando Pessoa & Co.*, Grove Press, 1998

It's not that existence is painful. (Some find it to be so, but shut up, it's not your turn right now.) It's that it is not as good as we can imagine. Not even close. To shear off daydreams from life and live only in a blissful recognition of *what* is would be a great loss. Life's nourishment is found between those ledger entries when we have the chance to dream something else.

Of course, Pessoa lived his life this way, endlessly inventing new persons who had their own biographies, personalities, interests, and writing styles. They wrote to each other about each other, and sometimes about Pessoa. Pessoa invented soccer leagues and asylums for them. In each idle moment, and there were many, new worlds and new people poured out from his mind in bewildering complexity and detail. His daydreams were far richer than anything he found in what some call life.

"Give me monotony—" Soares declares, "the dull repetition of the same old days, today an exact copy of yesterday—while my observant soul enjoys the fly that flits past my eyes and distracts me, the laughter that drifts up from I'm not sure which street, the liberation I feel when it's time to close the office, and the infinite repose of a day off." The joy of a flitting fly (God, I hope that's metaphorical, somehow) or a loud bar laugh—and, perhaps, the stories it suggests—punctuates a change in the otherwise monotonous backdrop of our lives. An opportunity to engage in a bit of fantasy allows us to truly live, in contrast to what we get paid to do. (That's some Marx thrown in, no charge.)

I have found, for example, that I enjoy going into the office, partly because I like the people there, but also because if I put in a full day of thoroughly monotonous work, sheer word-processed drudgery, then I have the great joy of coming home and—and here I know I am supposed to say "lose myself in novels and poetry" or something impressively artsy like that, but in fact I will say—playing fantasy video games. I am a barbarian, a world leader, a tomb raider. (Pessoa, far more impressively, manufactured his own virtual realities.) Staying home all day and playing these games would not be nearly as pleasurable as escaping into them from between two ledger entries. I live, I work, I *monotonize* so that the escape is so much better.

And I hasten to add (lest anyone think favorably of me) that it's not as if I feel I am doing valuable work during the day, and that I am somehow *earning the right* to have some mindless fun. No, I am free from any illusion of earning anything through my allegedly meaningful labor. I value the worthless crap I do because it is monotonous and makes the pleasure of escape all the greater. I'm pretty sure that's what Soares/Pessoa was/were getting at.

Jason Irwin

Rooms of My Life

At night I become a lost child wandering from room to room,
laying my hands on the counter tops, the kitchen table,

the cupboard full of ladles, as if with their mere touch
I could find that part of me that's died.

The Prodigal Son set out to find a life of fortune.
Among the hogs he saw a blinding light.

Today, rain pours down on the city of yellow bridges.
I sit thinking of the dead who fill these rooms

like so many books and furniture. It's a comfort sometimes,
to read certain novels again & again, to sit in familiar chairs,

to run my fingers over the frayed upholstery, the wood grain,
the grooves wrought by the carpenter's lathe.

Expansion as Relief
for Fernando Pessoa

All it takes to make a mirror is sliding
a coat of silver nitrate down a pane of glass.
Then: there may be two of you.

How to replicate again?
Simply crack the mirror and
place a piece on either side of you.

Then the multitude
      which becomes you
will march single-file
      beside you.

Onward, tiny spines!
Seen from above
like a perfect pattern
shining itself around.

As with facsimiles, each copy grows hazier;
each edge puckers into a blur.

Soon even
the deepest nesting center
of yourself,
where these other selves
collide and recollect,

becomes thick and watery
like a delta, a rich threshold.

But hear this:

    I know how achieving unison can
    begin to feel like anxious swarming

    I know how easy it is
    to knot up the listening with thought.

    I know what it is to melt off the maddening lull
    with the motion of reproduction,

    the consolation of forward and backward time
    being indistinguishable for even an instant.

    I know what it is to have shadows of yourself
    you'd rather not account for.

    I know the faith and doubt to which catastrophes lead.

I, too, have tucked each experience away in an envelope, and then,
    when the pocket of paper is outgrown, a trunk:
          the sensation like
          dropping pennies
          down a well, hopeful and
          wasteful at once.

I know the allure of saying,
"just one more," and "again" ...

I know the bare economy of loneliness.

As each heteronym is born,
a hiss sounds, like a train uncoupling.

I, too, have felt such lightness on my own engine.

To become singular again requires time and
patience while the mirrors fade and warp,
collect damage on their delicate backings.

However invisible the legend,
I promise you,
the power of the asymmetries
aligning into a gorgeous center
has been glowing steadily.

And I can tell you this:
    You will always have more eyes than mouths
    and there will always be more which goes unsaid.

George Kalamaras

Fernando Pessoa, 1923

There was never a joy like *any-human-pain*. Fernando Pessoa would cough tiny sparkling goldfish onto his hanky, asking if we could see the brilliant rain. Once, I passed him on the street, but he did not recognize me. He was busy reciting lines from Jack Spicer, though he had not yet been born. I watched him hand the grocer an apple, asking if the Tibetans were defeated yet by the Red Chinese. If the invasion of 1951 had already happened or if it was yet to come sometime after the 1930s. *History,* he said, *is never sequential. All time is distortion.* There was a calm even in his most agitated stance, as if all the death of the world were his one day to obliterate.

Twenty-three reis, the grocer replied. *I sell them in proportion to your body weight.*

Okay, she said, the woman next to him, with the opium eyes. *How much then to kill me?*

I swear Pessoa rubbed her left wrist with his own veins of deep blue sleep and trembled right there like a fluttering map before the oranges.

Lisbon, he replied, with a tuberculous cough not unlike the thunderous exaggerated ease of underwater speech. *Mozambique. Portuguese Guinea,* he continued. *Prayer flags and incense and tiny blessèd bells.* Then finally, *This avocado about to make me whole.*

Then he stumbled toward the bus, saying something about *sadness* and *green green hope* and *Rilke's unseen throat-of-a-bride* and *starlight confiscating that contiguous particle of Brahms*. Just out of earshot, on the bus's step, he almost turned toward me, his hook of a nose pointing down toward some great stirring that struggled to fiercely ache forth from the gravel or pebble or bricklayer's brick—there, his foot in mid-air poised, wing-tipped and polished, as if to leave this world, black and shiny, for some future, some past, undisclosed other.

Charles Cutler, Dan Mahoney & Gaby Gordon-Fox, eds.

Into the Moist
for Fernando Pessoa

He swore that he never kept sheep, that the mournful lyric of
his loneliness was a pale green scarf and dimming hips
on a porch.
He had made multiple names, not just *Álvaro de Campos* or
Bernardo Soares, but skin sores like *foreskin boy* and
Portuguese pain in the jungles of Brazil.

It was the season of salt. It was always the season of salt.
Even the sheets absorbed all his nights of lurking and strength.

If you want dampness as a fierce form of fatality, he told me, *then
count the small deaths of the wrist.*
Examine the blood map that enters and leaves the body at once.

He had inherited the blue-veined anxiety of the topography
of a broken star.
Sure, he had multiple shames, not just *Ricardo Reis* or *Alberto
Caeiro*, but agonies sequestered as boils, lancings in
the shape of *touch-me-where-it-hurts-because-it- hurts-
all-over*, and *write-my-biography-but-do-so-sadly-while-
counting-backwards- to-one.*

Even dead birds spilled from his ear, jungle-like, into the moist.
Even the sheets, which absorbed his solitude, grew thick with
the almost-love of so much utter clutch.

Fernando Pessoa Might Call My Body True

It was like lighting my tongue on fire.
The kerosene rag could not be used for the monthly blood.

It was like entering my leopard body, absorbing the sag of each
    dark star as I muscle-twitched my paw-patched self
    bramble-wise across the savannah toward freedom
    and remorse.
The blood bag could not fill even an empty bell or the silver of
    a word I struggled to maintain.

Sure, Fernando Pessoa might call the cave of my body true,
    might send me out onto the parched streets of Lisbon
    begging bread.
Of course, his hatband contained secret words, phrases like
    cave-light in my mouth and *Fedora Pessoa is a bowl of*
    frightened soup and *Stir my blood lightly with a stick.*

I lost a shoe and closed the night as we almost spoke of
    Portugal and pain, of the sandaled sadness of throat
    slash for chalice and spice in ports as colonially close
    as Goa and Malacca.
Anything could bleed, he told me, *if you speak it just right. Any*
    mouth could be sewn shut with the awful alignment of
    saffron and scripture.

He showed me a photo of a zebra in foal, of blacks and whites
among the scorched ash of bamboo.
He showed me an Indian woman from Goa who refused
baptism, forced to watch her husband denuded, his
penis stuffed into his own mouth.

And we wept together as if *both* lit by kerosene.
And the tongue of our mouth was Christlike, if not exact.

And we cried like a child who has lost her star.
And I held Fernando's hand and felt the tender agony of release.

Ariana-Sophia Kartsonis

Fernando Pessoa, I Salute You All!

> *I want to take off with you, I want to go away with you, with all of you at once.*
> —Álvaro Campos

Let's pinkie promise never to part
ourselves out just because we know what it means
to be many-ed as a hotel corridor.
Each chamber of our hearts
contains a different guest,
and as the case may be, Fernando, Fernando,
it's hard to say who you are
when everywhere there's evidence of someone else's
aftershave, someone's cigarette left burning
in the ashtray in another wing of you.
Nonetheless, you're my favorite octopod
and I'd run away with you, Baby.
We could be in Sicily by Sunday
some of ourselves wandering the city
before that early light gets all used up.
Others of us sleeping in or fingerprinting
the crowd which is just you and me, which is
just fine, since I'm aware that you're aware
that mankind's just another way of saying: there's nobody home.

You'll know what I mean when I tell you that I've been known
to find myself on a metro train inside myself where one
or the other of me has already taken the last seat

and this ride, yet again, I stand, holding the strappy
thing that makes me feel like a side of beef hanging heavy
and jostled from the walls while my city, my city, smears
the side windows and I'm just trying to stay upright.
The train is preferable to a crowd
of us packed into my little vehicle of catastrophe.

If one of us drives too fast in the rain
how many of us slide into oblivion?

You're all about the static, the stations between stations. You,
you are every radio in every hotel
in all the cities that are you and you again.

I'll give myself a heteronym
the same as my beloved's favorite poet.
Every final couplet will read the same:
How do you like me now, Love?
How do you like me now?

I've had some time to think it over and
I'd like to wash your back in Portuguese,
comb your hair in Spanish, address
your every eyelash by a pet name.

The sky is made of cardboard.
I adore corrugation: the ups and downs,
a sheet of cardboard's inner life:
zig-zag and heart monitor and some dark honey

eyes, you've got there Fern (may I call you
Fern?) casting your vertebraed shadow everywhere.
I'd follow those tracks, I'd take
that train across the country and write every day
to the man who first checked your book out of the library
for me, and who loved me, like God's greatest maniac,
until I kissed the magic from his top hat
and now, there's nothing I can do but wait
for the previews to end and hope, hope
the feature film will begin and at least one of me
will have even a bit part. Therein lies the problem
with leading men, Fernando, the screen darkens
and attitude gets thrown. Let's take a bus of us
to the drive-in movie starring you,
co-starring you, written, produced, edited
by you: my gaffer, my key grip, my best boy
electric, my soundtrack, my all.

You, me and Jesus, Baby, we're lousy with disciples.
Mine drag me around by the scruff of the neck
and when I ask whether it's bitch-love or cruelty
that motivates this mode of travel, they don't say a word.

Here, there, everywhere you. And isn't that my hoop skirt?
Your mouth makes moths cry. Little life, won't you wear
me again like you did last fall? We held ourselves up to each other
like lighters at a rock concert and then the swaying started
and all the little people in my head stood up and did the wave.
If you take the stage, I might just shatter.

Charles Cutler, Dan Mahoney & Gaby Gordon-Fox, eds.

Some nights some trees become candelabras and I can almost see your brilliance thrumming an octopus of torchlight: each star toasting the others, each other toasting the stars.

Joy Ladin

Fossilized Happiness

I trace your suggestively regular curves
    with dangerously
ungloved hands, violating protocol
    and decades of discipline
to stroke a schist

of dubious provenance,
    a find from a bin amassed
by one of those tireless Victorians
    who destroyed so much of the past;
whose deformities

I precisely predict
    in a still-unpublished paper that almost swayed
the editors of NATURE;
    whose existence suggests

Homo sapiens descends
    from a genus no reputable anthropologist
had the heart to imagine:
    Homo felicitatus,
innately happy man.

I can almost hear her now:
    Science is desire
that's learned to present

   its least-tenable conclusions
as logical premises." That

was the sort of thing she said,
  often over wine, often
in a whisper
  as she cradled my head.
I'd like to ask her

where she'd fit you in:
  a fossil of a feeling
that refused to disappear
  when the flow of mud cut off your host's
supply of oxygen.

We are neither of us intact.
  The white-gloved lord who dubbed you
"some kind of dinosaur egg"
  couldn't understand
how hard you are to distinguish

from your environment. Crushed
  the lobe that could have answered
vexed and vexing questions,
  leaving an irregular gash
where hypotheses sprout

and wither like grass:
  how you fit the skull

In the Footsteps of a Shadow

of the dominant hominid; what
    advantage you conferred; and
(a purely personal note)

why you have the firm, shy curve
    of a budding breast.
You can open up to me,
    we're not so different:
two putty-colored forms

that survived by assimilating
    what destroyed us. Evidence
for the theory that says
    a life can be constructed
from depressions, skull fragments and flints,

that the prints of a walk on the shore
    of a sea that no longer exists
can tell us two mature examples
    of homo this or that
surprised each other here, and here, and here

prognathous, kissed—

    *

We met in Athens, at a symposium,
    stalled in an elevator between
an anxious paleo-psychologist

and an outraged Skinnerian.
She smelled of Queen Anne's lace

and said she found my work
    "a stimulating irritant."
She was the only philosopher
    I could ever stand.
We had lunch together—dinner—

in the morning we traded danish—
    debating her contention
that science is merely a wish
    to drape in a consoling shape
the immense and meaningless.

Ridiculous! I thought, and told her—
    it was true—that I was fascinated.
The conference had canceled my talk
    but I felt like the lucky stiff
bumped from the expedition

who, among unlabeled crates,
    discovers a whole new genus.
After the conference, we corresponded.
    I was restless, dissatisfied
with my work, the evanescent hints that you—

or rather, the unsubstantiated region I called
    "the organ of happiness"—

In the Footsteps of a Shadow

had somehow both atrophied and grown
   so hideously efficient
that in modern *sapiens*,

in whom you're reduced
   to a few stray folds,
ecstasies which once took weeks
   are processed in a matter of seconds.
I had to see her again.

I took her into the basement
   of a world-famous museum,
down among the fibulae and flints,
   the painfully simple ornaments
from the earliest burial chambers.

We carbon-dated; I showed her how
   a gouged black schist implied
both a conscious purpose and a mind
   that knew it would never achieve it.
I don't believe in God

but I showed her the evidence
   that something is struggling up through us,
something that needs a brain twice the size
   of the one you nestled in
to reduce the universe

to what she called
  "our cocoon of lies and wishes."
She said like all religious men
  I thought I'd find the meaning of life
by rooting among the dead.

What if I have, I countered.
  Stop rooting, then, she said.
Sometimes, when I close my eyes, I imagine
  unearthing her skeleton:
first the knees

drawn slightly up, then legs, pelvis, ribs,
  the remarkably eloquent calcium
suggesting the languorous stretch
  of a lover on a rainy morning
trying to get out of bed;

and then, though my life's work is based
  on the fact that it isn't there, I imagine
inside the cranium
  a mottled lump that looks like you
and was our happiness.

  *

I piece her together
  from whispers and chips.
It's me she's buried in.

In the Footsteps of a Shadow

Like a Neolithic midden,
I'm full of half-burned scraps.

She worried about money in the shower.
   She wrote with a fine-point pen.
She found an erotic satisfaction
   in shaving the tiny hairs
that point like a sign made of fur

down the back of my neck.
   Asleep, she looked 9 or 10.
Once, for 16 hours straight,
   she stared at a vein in her hand;
that was the closest she ever came

to conducting an empirical test.
   She claimed Kant would never have died a virgin
if she'd been around back then.
   I never believed that she believed
half the things she said.

For two or three years,
   I thought she was having an affair.
Then, during a kiss that seemed designed
   for another pair of lips,
I realized the man she wanted

was one who didn't exist,
    and started digging deeper and deeper,
until I discovered him.

        *

Summer's begun to end.
    I hear one cricket
scraping his legs
    above the buzz of fluorescents.
I wonder what he feels—

A thickening of the blood?
    an ache in his bowing legs?
Will he mate only once in his life?
    Will he know when he's met his match?
How can he stand it, night after night,

in that vibrating carapace?
    Maybe she was right, and all this—
the fluoroscopes, the magnifying eyes, the imaging resonance—
    are like his scraping legs,
summoning bodies in the dark

that cannot answer back.
    Strip-streep, strip-streep:
his summons repeats
    like the Intensive Care machine
she mistook for me

In the Footsteps of a Shadow

when, with a fever of a hundred and three
   and tubes in her marvelous hands,
she tried to say
   either how much she'd loved
or hated—

I couldn't quite hear which.
   So many machines
to track our hearts
   and yet we have no test
to tell us how we felt

last night; last year;
   when we curled on the floor of a cave;
when the elevator stalled;
   when her kidneys failed.
All we have is a lump of stone

that held its oddly suggestive form
   while a million summers passed,
crickets sang,
   and hominids developed
the capacity to ask

why the past
   like a badly assembled skull
is riddled with tiny cracks.
   That's what she would have said, pointing out
that my lab is a mess

and that I'm blushing, brushing
    an inch-long stone
with naked fingertips;
    that my lips are moving—
Prayer? she'd ask—

and that, no matter what I wish,
    no one else is here.
Go home, she'd say.
    She couldn't understand.
In this profession, a successful life

is one that ends intact, preserved
    by a properly staged disaster
for ten thousand generations
    until graduate students with horsehair brushes
exhume it bit by bit.

You were a success.
    Even when your skull
was crushed beyond recognition,
    you waited,
preserving your essential structure

for someone who could grasp
    what it meant for happiness
to outlast bone and flesh.
    High in the tree
from which we all descend,

In the Footsteps of a Shadow

you waited while we shambled,
   slope-shouldered then erect,
and our thumbs began to oppose us
   and our foreheads grew immense,
singing like a cricket in the dark,

trying to call us back.

Philip Levine

You Are You

> *I am me.*
> —Pessoa

Once upon a time—How now can I begin
like that? It's June 30, 2000, it's morning
still cool although the murderous heat is waiting
impatiently in the high branches of the eucalyptus.
You shake your head no. Heat is an abstraction.
Those are four black crows, you insist, the same ones
I heard in my sleep last night and which were transformed
in the theater of dreams into two congressmen
proclaiming out of both sides of their mouths.

Let's get back to the weather. The four crows
are certainly there, though two have descended
from the tree to circle over a faded red Toyota
in the parking lot of the Fig Garden Lady's Association
as though it were part living animal, part vegetable,
instead of steel, plastic, rubber, glass, whatever.
It belongs to the middle-aged gardener in coveralls
who comes once a month to trim the hedges, to plant
fresh blooms beside the walkway, and to water the parking lot.

His first name is Italo. He has short, bristly gray hair
under his Giants' cap, and though he's lived in California
more than half his life he knows sunshine and water
will not make concrete blossom. Tomorrow the ladies

will gather, the older ones arriving in Lincolns and Caddies,
the younger ones in sleek imports. "I've got my orders," says Italo
shaking his head that's solidly balanced on wide shoulders.
"Once upon a time," he told me back in 1982,
"I told them watering this was a waste of water."

People do speak that way, they say what's on their minds
cogently and they do so without theatrical gestures
while holding a hose in one hand and a cigarette
in the other. That is the beauty of syntax, rhetoric,
of language itself. I am me. You are you.
The four crows have come to earth to stump about
the parked Toyota and peck for final truths or worms
while at last the sun clears the giant eucalyptus
to cast its shimmering welcome on the wet concrete.

Annie Lighthart

In the Hour Favorable to Transformation

In the hour favorable to transformation, the heart
has no quarter. A man turns a corner, another
watches him turning, and time remains
ambiguous and odd.
What is not in danger of contingency and loss?

Two sides of a corner meet only at their edge,
as a yellow-stubbed daisy core
meets emptiness in wind.

Even the leaf has rivers
dividing its bright skin.
The heart sees this and has no quarter:
it is not a green stalk, it has too many uses,
it refuses the confluence of song.

Johnny Lorenz

Oxcart

When I was no longer
any use,
they unfastened me
from the animal,
removed my wheels
and threw me
into a ditch by the road.
It's unclear to me
if I'm an oxcart still.
Everything moves
and changes.
I might become wood
for a fire. I might
become the fire.
If only my life
were human, I'd believe
in the names of things.

Charles Cutler, Dan Mahoney & Gaby Gordon-Fox, eds.

Daniel Mahoney

We Are Fernando

Hello

I am Fernando

I am four hundred

I have come to ask for Maria José some cooking oils

I spoke yesterday as perhaps another one

I am sorry

I am Fernando

Do you have some aspect of chicken for me to go with

I am four hundred and hungry

I am me and the others are also

We are here and here

Each is called like me

We are Fernando

In the Footsteps of a Shadow

So many of us

Do you have coffee

We are from a place of water

Each one out of water

All of us together

We are four hundred

If you have wine with you

I and my others and Maria José

We are another time in this room

We remember

This table with coffee and cigarettes

We return each day

Become more

And more ourselves

Charles Cutler, Dan Mahoney & Gaby Gordon-Fox, eds.

Dennis Maloney

Pessoa Café, Amsterdam

Between the streets
of red lights
and Central Station,
down the alley
past a canal, we find the
Pessoa Café.

Ah, the first minutes
in cafes of new cities!
We raise a glass to
 all those voices
we carry within,
but there are real
conversations to be had.

All of us see
ghosts before us.
How many masks
do we wear, the
waitress, the cook,
patrons sitting at
the other tables?

Pessoa said I'm an ascetic
in the religion of myself.
A cup of coffee, a cigarette,
and my dreams substitute

In the Footsteps of a Shadow

quite well for the
universe and its stars.

Off in a corner,
he starts to fidget,
orders another drink,
pulls some paper
from his pocket,
scribbles down verses
on the back of a handbill,
fragments, teetering
on the brink of illegibility.

Charles Cutler, Dan Mahoney & Gaby Gordon-Fox, eds.

CLINT MARGRAVE

Pessoa Died a Virgin

They say the closest relationship
he ever had with a woman
led to a mental collapse that
almost put him in a madhouse.
Whatever the cause, it scared him
so much, he never got involved
with another one. Maybe it was
the pipe she hid because she
thought he smoked too much,
or the way she kept punning
his name in French to mean "nobody."
Certainly it didn't help he made her
pray for one of his heteronyms,
and wrote her a letter that said,
"My life revolves around my
literary work.... Everything else
is only of secondary interest."
Or maybe it was those "impossible"
adolescent loves, still engrained
in his memory, with their
"deceitful affection," their "shrewd caresses,"
 that continued to aggrieve him,
create "cosmic cataclysms" in his soul,
push him to retreat inside
the imagination, teach him early
on what so many of the trampled
only wish they'd known.

Cate Marvin

Little Poem That Tries

Little Poem That Tries likes to make pretend it is a land
where dislikes inform its borders, tells its knees to leave
if they won't stop kneeling, then announces it's time to

my Kentucky courthouse heart my credit counseling heart

clean house. Its orders come from the top, shudder their
way down, striking fear into the bowels of the lowliest
custodial workers. Appoints serial killers for its customs

my file for bankruptcy heart my long distance phone call

officials. Destroys its orange groves with a single dream.
Reenters the house, limping. Acquires an endless supply
of Xanax, believes it possible it is living inside a movie

heart my courtesy call heart my manual dial my I am dying

and when the sun calms down—if the fervent sun ever
calms itself down—it'll pat itself on the back, think how
much prettier the days are with the companion of a sun

heart my note in my throat tries and dies heart my Jersey

that kills: how in drought graves split open, cannot keep
their bones down. The land's heated disarray underneath
such violet skies; does it not remind one of a tangled sheet,

Turnpike heart my Divorce Court heart my small claims

how the pill of the past is easy enough to swallow once
it's crushed up, spoon-fed with such amorous light?
To gaze all day as the sun plays along a riot of graves ...

heart my service window heart my claimant heart my

rather a peaceful pastime, as if what's been said is truly
done. Though it never intended to undertake a coup, one
might conclude from the teary countenances of officials

hit my car heart my notarized heart my foreclosed heart

round the conference table that the Little Poem that Tries
was never right for this job in the first place. After it pats
its reader down, it slips into a hired car, makes itself *far*,

my unsubsidized loan heart my on loan and lonely heart

makes itself away. Now, the hot, purpling sky turns to fog.
All the scorched fields shrink below. The still stars above.
And Little Poem That Tries snows and snows and snows.

my how could you have hit the one nice thing I owned heart

Constance Rowell Mastores

Oxymoron

I would like to believe in the everyness
of things. In the universe and fiery stars.
In the warp-worlds. In the greater possibility
of that impossibility. In the huge seductiveness
burning outside my window. Every night
it winks at me. Every night, at odds, I stare at it
and write strange sentences on yellow tablets
that create their own kind of haphazard universe
upon the table. I read them like Rorschach test.
I see windmills. I tilt at them. I tilt at the universe
burning outside my window, dare it to make me
believe, to walk right up to me and announce
itself—shake me by the shoulder. *There is
in God, some say, a deep, but dazzling darkness.*

Charles Cutler, Dan Mahoney & Gaby Gordon-Fox, eds.

John T. Medeiros

faith

a portuguese man
who loves a man
is neither a man
nor portuguese
for he has been
too long away
that is what they say
yet they embrace pessoa
and shout he was their best
and erect a statue for him
on the busiest street
on the busiest hill
in lisbon, and when asked
why did sá-carneiro
succumb to strychnine
by his own hand
all they can offer is
he was an artist
haunted by his own soul
besides he lived in france
we are complex creatures
catholic miracles
pave our path
and we believe enough
to walk on our knees
and blame ourselves
when our beloved lady

In the Footsteps of a Shadow

of fatima passes us by
and we believe enough
in miracles like blood
raining from the sky
yet a portuguese man
who loves a man
is neither a man
nor portuguese

Charles Cutler, Dan Mahoney & Gaby Gordon-Fox, eds.

Christopher Merrill

Sagebrush
for Aleš Debeljak

These are the last days of its empire. No flags fly from its dead limbs, nor do its branches lost to age or blight bend in the wind. Only two outposts remain, two settlements of grey and green, in the largest house of which the general lifts his fork before casually signing marching orders for his starving troops. Here in a field of shrunken cabbages the asthmatic priest wakes in the night, gasping. Foot soldiers reach for their inhalers. Courtesans bronze their nails. In a world of whiskers and spent flowers there are always rumors of barbarians gathering beyond the barbed wire the prisoners strung across the last meadow on our maps. Even our bravest cartographer prefers the company of the general to wandering past that fence, though the general will never share his food. No doubt a messenger from the capital is already on his way to the first outpost, bearing orders for our retreat. Who will inherit the promise of these stiff limbs? Ants, grass, and wind. What is the price of wisdom here? Only the priest and prisoners can tell.

George Monteiro

Surface Noise

It scares me, this life
I can't face up to. In
fact, while I can't
entirely bring it off, I
do better facing it down.
I'm an aggressive son-
of-a-bitch, but it's a
touch-and-go existence
I allow myself. Or is it
the touch-and-go myself
that allows the other—
the me I am—this,
and only this much?
Who speaks for me now
or through me? Is it
Fernando Pessoa, his
orthonymic self, sporting
with me, or is it one
of his sweaty heteronyms
scraping out a horned-bottom
scapegoat, who can't, or
won't, cry foul?

Charles Cutler, Dan Mahoney & Gaby Gordon-Fox, eds.

Autobiography

Why set down in detail the life of
someone described once, not unfairly,
as 'the man who never was'? How
can you write the biography of one
who devised dozens of names for
pieces of himself when he did not,
would not or could not be himself
Better to set down your own auto-

biography or, better still, probe the life
of a neighbor, who'll probably not kill
you or thank you if and when he finds
out. Don't bother about the dates—
1888 (T. S. Eliot's and O'Neill's,
too) or 1935—and don't mention his
schooling, all of which, practically,
took place in South Africa, instruction

in English. Don't slip into the destructive
element by mentioning the death of
the father when he was five or six or
his mother's remarriage or the string
of children (some dying soon, others
outliving him) that filled his stepfather's
house in Durban, or that the family
doctor at the time fathered a poet, Roy

In the Footsteps of a Shadow

Campbell, who would follow our poet in
school (where he saw his predecessor's
name—or initials, I forget which—carved
on his desktop, he claimed). Forget his jobs,
back in Lisbon–boring beyond words—
setting up a print shop-publishing house (quick
failure), amanuensis (at the typewriter) for
various firms in the Baixa, librarianship up

the coast (oops, he didn't get that job; there
was another candidate), and unremunerated
projects, such as inventing a translation
typewriter, a *planta* for Lisbon, etc. etc.
Editing *Orpheu* and *Athena* fill out the list,
glorious now for those who continue to
count on such things. Death at forty-seven
but not before winning a second first prize

(or was it a first-time second prize—nobody
remembers, nor does it matter) and not before
recognition by the swaggering literary boys
in Coimbra. Death at night in the French hospital,
the English hospital but a stone's throw away
from his bedroom—nice touch to a life such as
his, but only filler. The seemingly bottomless
trunk, left behind, that raises an eyebrow but soon

becomes just the fetish, all-enveloping for those
who won't recognize it as such. Posthumous

Charles Cutler, Dan Mahoney & Gaby Gordon-Fox, eds.

publication of stuff he stuffed away to bear witness to a life still unlived—the real story but hardly the stuff of a biography. Then the heteronyms, each with things of this world, but that's another story, not this one. I've forgotten Ophelia; but so did he—twice.

A Conceit

It's as if each heteronym was a specialized self-storage unit, a warehouse, if you will, for his varied and contrarian thoughts. Some of these lockers he filled beyond their capacity, others he left half-filled, and still others he abandoned with little or nothing in them. His followers mostly play at storage wars, a game in which each of them has paid nothing to look into a black box, jammed with ciphers.

Charles Cutler, Dan Mahoney & Gaby Gordon-Fox, eds.

Riding a Metaphor

What is the opposite of shards, which, after all, are just pieces broken off some sort of whole showing, nevertheless, some traces of DNA? So from any one piece an archeologist should be able to discern the whole and image it forth for all to see. This can be done by a team of apparatchiks. So, too, might the shards of my baú be arranged to body forth my mind, by way of model, as I cold never have known it. Ah, but pieces in this case are more like bits of color, seen beautifully in a kaleidoscope one time and only once, always to be turned over, ever so slightly, into another pattern, just as beautiful and just as unique. After all, I needn't tell you, a mind is not a pot, nor, shattered, its pieces shards. You can no more have a unifying theory (that will hold for more than an instant) than you can rest at will. Stop for a sip of water, not to quench a thirst, but to celebrate in satisfaction, and the kaleidoscope shifts ever so slightly and its dance of color and light once again becomes something, of temporary permanence. That's how I approached what I saw, what I felt, what I thought. It's but a seahorse, and that's about it.

Stanley Moss

An Exchange of Hats

I will my collection of hats,
straw the Yucatan, fez Algiers 1935,
Russian beaver, Irish fisherman's knit,
collapsible silk opera, a Borsalino,
to a dead man,
the Portuguese poet, my dear Fernando,
who, without common loyalty,
wrote under seven different names
in seven different styles.
He was a man of many cafés,
a smoker and non-smoker.
His poets came to live in Lisbon,
had different sexual preferences,
histories and regional accents.

Still their poems had a common smell
and loneliness that was Fernando's.
His own character
was to him like ink to a squid,
something to hide behind.
What did it matter, writing in Portuguese
after the First World War? The center was Paris,
the languages French and English.

In Lisbon, workers on the street corner were arguing
over what was elegance, the anarchist manifesto,
the trial of Captain Artur Carols de Barros

found guilty of "advocating circumcision"
and teaching Marranos no longer to enter church
saying "When I enter I adore neither wood nor stone
but only the Ancient of Days who rules all."

Eirin Moure

Notes in Recollection

In me, there appeared my master.
—Fernando Pessoa to Adolfo Casais Monteiro about Alberto Caeiro and March 8,1914, the day he wrote some 30 of the 49 poems of *The Keeper of Sheep,* "in a sort of ecstasy."

The anonymity of the civic grid parallels the anonymity of fields. When I was a child, I was also a bird. A bird and a fisher. Then I spent a winter on Winnett Avenue in Toronto where a small creek crosses, nameless, flowing under the road into Cedarvale ravine near the Phil White Arena. A manhole cover, *the real McCoy,* marks its passage. A portal, round, of *fer forgé.* In Montréal these covers would say *Montréal égouts,* or *aqueduc,* or *égout pluvial,* in accordance with their function; in Toronto they read *McCoy,* after their foundry. Or just bear a year. 1965. Beneath them, I started to find creeks, riding my bike that spring; for on a bike, you can hear the water. Travelling up Wychwood past the old shut streetcar barns, the sound of Taddle Creek can be followed all the way up to Vaughan Road before it's lost. And on a bike,[1] you're instantly aware of topography. At night from downtown, the craggy Lake Iroquois shore just above Davenport in Toronto is a dark line: to rise out of the vanished lake into it is to enter a lung. In such a place, I first translated the words of Portuguese poet Fernando Pessoa. Or, more properly, Alberto Caeiro.

---

1. In a car, you can't hear creeks. Besides, a car's nearly impossible in the warren of one-way streets designed to prevent through traffic to the truncated Allen Expressway.

It started on March 20, 2000. In Providence, Rhode Island, I decided not to read anything for five days and just think. But I couldn't help it. Back in Toronto, I read *Garrison Creek* in brass letters in the pavement outside the liquor store on St. Clair Avenue and could see its trajectory southward to the lake, under an avenue. I knew what the No Frills parking lot had been, then. It was the ugly urban pastoral of my Calgary childhood, creek territory.

Later I opened Alberto Caeiro's *O Guardador de Rebanhos*, a bilingual version (tr. Honig & Brown) I'd bought in Providence on my first day of not-reading because it was red. I looked at the verso side and realized: *I can read Portuguese.*

Whoosh!

It was as if studying Galician had created new neurons in my head. So to amuse and scare myself, I translated a short poem, altering posture and voice, and sometimes (thus) words, but still staying "true" to the poem. A few pages and days later, I realized Pessoa had entered Toronto, living a pastoral life in Toronto's not-quite-vanished original topographies. In me, there appeared my master. Finally, I could feel joy. I found Taddle Creek in Wychwood Park. Then I found the creek that crosses Winnett Avenue just below where I lived. After I found the creeks, I lived alongside them.

And Alberto Caeiro came with me. I translated Pessoa by responding to him as a person. I, a person, and Pessoa, a person. For in Portuguese, *pessoa* is person. I just read the Pessoan poem line, then wrote my line, or read a few lines, then wrote mine. It was abrupt, direct, total.

At the same time, I couldn't write too many at once. It set my heart murmur going. Besides, I was afraid of responding to the context of what I'd already done, and I wanted to respond only to the Pessoa lines, using the context of my own corporeal position in the world north of Vaughan Road. In just over a week I'd translated some 30 of the 49 poems, in a sort of ecstasy. It was a form of prayer I lit each day, a vigil candle.

Toronto's Garrison Creek once ran down from where I'd found it at No Frills (that chaotic cut-rate supermarket where I walked to buy food), through Christie Pits, then continued south, in the ravine system still visible as parks here and there. Where Harbord Street crosses that ravine, between Montrose and Grace, there was once a big bridge. When they filled in the ravine, they buried the bridge too. I unburied it with Pessoa.

A last note: I see this book as translation, as faithful, even if different. That's why it appears in a bilingual edition with the Portuguese originals—my deflections of Pessoa's texts are thus *visible*, even if you do not read Portuguese. I want this book to be judged not just as my poetry but as translations of Pessoa. Trans-e-lations. Trans-eirin-elations. Transcreations. A *sheep's vigil, of a fervent person.*

Charles Cutler, Dan Mahoney & Gaby Gordon-Fox, eds.

I. What, me, guard sheep
for Phil Hall

What, me, guard sheep
I made that up; this is poetry.
It's my soul that's sheepish
Knows wind and sun
Grabs onto every Season and follows, looking.
Nature's peaceful today; it's empty
and it's my pal.
But it saddens me: what if sunset
turns my lights out too
when the parking lot goes cold
and nightfall's butterfly presses at my body,
glass.

But being sad isn't all bad,
it's fair enough and natural
What else is a soul for?
It's so sure it exists
when the hand cuts flowers, it doesn't cry out.

Like the racket of the mail truck
Coming around the curve of the avenue
My thoughts are happy.
Yet simply thinking this makes me glum,
For if they weren't happy, there'd be more variety:
Instead of being happy and glum
They'd be joyful and happy. What the heck.

In the Footsteps of a Shadow

Thinking bugs me, like walking in the rain
When the bus goes by, a huge wind splattering greasy water.

Ambitions and desires? My head's wet.
Being a poet isn't an ambition,
it's a version of being alone.

And if I sometimes want
(I'm making this up!) to be a lamb,
(Or to be the whole flock
with a flock's funny gait on the hillside,
one leg shorter than the other)
It's just that I feel what I write at sunset
or when a cloud's hand shields the light
And my neighbour goes in, after cutting his lawn.

When I sit writing poems
or when walking Vaughan Road or along the alley
I write poems in my head, because that's how I think.
The pen I hold is my shepherd's crook,
And I see my own figure
on the crest of Bathurst,
Guarding my flock and viewing my ideas
Or guarding my ideas and viewing my flock
and smiling half-goofy like my friend Phil.

Hello to you, Phils of the future:
I take my hat off to you.
Look, I'm in my own doorway on Winnett

across from another parking lot.
I hope you've got sun,
and rain when you need it,
And that in your houses
you've a chair and a window that opens
where you've just read this: it's a poem.
And that reading it makes you think
I'm a natural—
For example, an ancient tree that thrives on a buried creek,
Where children plop down when they're sick of playing,
And wipe the heat off their sticky foreheads
with the sleeve of a t-shirt,
their striped t-shirts now wet in my striped shade.

II. My sight's sharp as a sunflower

My sight's sharp as a sunflower.
I walk up Winnett to Vaughan Road all the time
Looking left and right
And sometimes looking over my shoulder ...
And what I see every moment
Is what no one's seen before me,
And, as such, I just let myself go ...
I feel like a child in a t-shirt
Amazed by just being born
and realizing "hey, I'm born" ...
I feel myself born at every moment
Into the World's eternity of the New ...

I believe in the world and in marigolds,
Because I see them. But I don't think on it
For thinking can't understand ...
The world isn't made for us to think in (thinking is eye-sore)
But to gaze at, and to harken ...

I've no philosophy: I've feelings ...
I don't talk of Nature knowing what it is,
But just because I love it, and I love it "as such,"
For a lover never knows that which she loves
nor why, nor what love is ...

Charles Cutler, Dan Mahoney & Gaby Gordon-Fox, eds.

To love is to abide in innocence,
hey, I'm still amazed ...
And I'm 45, just pulling my t-shirt on ...

XVI. What I'd give for my life to be my neighbour's old car

What I'd give for my life to be my neighbour's old car
Roaring pointlessly every morning on Winnett,
that later returns more quietly
near evening, along the same avenue.

I wouldn't need to cling to hope—I'd only need wheels ...
I'd get old without wrinkles and without grey hair ...
When the time comes that I'm useless, they'd just sell my tires
and mop up the oil I leaked on the driveway,

And I'd lie on my roof, my hot roof, at the bottom of a hot gully.

XXXII. Late yesterday in the Agora ...

Yesterday I went downtown, and came right back again.
A guy was pontificating in the crowded subway,
Addressing even me;
He spoke of justice and Third-World debt
And of workers who suffer
And of endless labour and the hungry,
And the rich who want a flat tax for us all (read *them*).

Spotting me, he saw my eyes well up
And thought he'd touched me
With all his hate and *soi-disant* compassion.

(But I wasn't really listening. What's the teeming city to me
And people's endless suffering?
If they lived on Winnett, they'd feel better.
All the world's evils come from confrontation,
Whether wanting to do good or bad.
Soul, sky and earth are all that's needed;
To crave more is to lose this, and be miserable.)

And I, I was thinking
As the people's self-appointed friend went on,
(And this is what brought me to tears)
How the screech of the subway's braking
Was so unlike the one-way traffic on Winnett
Where flowers and creek go to adore

In the Footsteps of a Shadow

And my neighbour drives his car backwards—
at least he's pointed in the right direction.

(Lucky I'm not made for doing good
And just have the natural egoism of flowers,
The egoism of creeks that follow waterways even underground,
Concentrating without plans
On flourishing and coursing.
And this is the sole aim of *world*,
This—to exist in the clear—
And do so, without thinking.)

And the guy fell silent, exiting onto Front Street,
gazing dumbstruck to the west, toward Mississauga.
That's where sunset blazes in Toronto!
Maybe he senses there's a creek there ... but he'll never find it ...

Charles Cutler, Dan Mahoney & Gaby Gordon-Fox, eds.

DAVID RADAVICH

Split Infinities
on Fernando Pessoa

How many selves
are a self?

How many clouds make
a sky, stones
keep a riverbed?

Do the petals recognize
each other
in their scent?

And yet the bees
still hover,

sun breaks
sea-mist open,

the moon drinks barley
over the fields.

How many names
point in the wrong direction.

Even God has trouble
with prophets

hiding
in their caves.

Now I see
a wily carnival

as arms and legs move
earthward
on dancing stilts.

Charles Cutler, Dan Mahoney & Gaby Gordon-Fox, eds.

Matthew Rasmussen

Overnight

> *I am one of my perceptions.*
> —Fernando Pessoa

The tube of lipstick
I buried in the yard

grew a garden of mouths.
The mouths sprouted

bodies that walked
into my house,

pushed me right out
of myself. They lived

my life branchingly,
like I was a sheet

of glass turned back
into sand.

Jennifer Silke Ray

de Campos Mentis

Materiality, it laughs at me.
I hear it snicker around street corners
with every fall I take ... pratfall, really,
considering the comedy contract clause
I dreamt I signed before taking the meat-spool;
e.g, my trip is canceled for revolution,
dashing unexamined elitist dreams
and theoretical money—"Idiot!," I say,
"why'd I attempt to visit the Egypt that exists
when the only true Egypt resides in my soul?"
Engage such flickering hijinks at one's peril, yet
engagement's the pinnacle, any deb knows—
swinging around that finger, bouncing light
at bleary, double-blind-experiment eyes

Charles Cutler, Dan Mahoney & Gaby Gordon-Fox, eds.

Elizabeth Robinson

Having Words

You, perhaps, only wanted to know how many words
fit on a page,

but these variables are contingent on season.
And in this heat the words slide right off

the surface of the paper. Meaning to touch you,
I found my hand full instead of oily letters.

I could feel by the curl of the page that
your discouragement infused the writing

entirely. Holding this sample, damp
and tattered with the grease of summer rain, I was at an impasse

myself. Do you realize that you talk incessantly
about breathing, about what it's like

to pull something into your lungs? But suddenly, what had
always been as tiresome as hearing a family member

recite his dreams became
real for me: the thickness of the air, the muggy downpour,
all played cinematically before the both of us. That is,

the idea of the page seemed laughable while
the pure liquid viscosity of what we slurped in as
"breath" ran full with syllables. The number of words,

the exact delight of them, was exactly what I did know.
Sultry, unglued,

I threw your document away. I no longer needed
to count breaths on your behalf. Nor ask how to persist

through the day's scorch. My one sigh was that precise.

Charles Cutler, Dan Mahoney & Gaby Gordon-Fox, eds.

"a deeper breathing with other lungs"

I knew air was a collage
and my body a rebus that drove
my breath through the maze of symbols
until I stood
dizzy,
at an intersection.

Strange, how the sound of images and
automobiles whirring by was muffled.
Now I hear nothing but the oceanic slough of air
in my ears as I inhale
and inhale. I hadn't
wanted my solitude interrupted,
and solitude's own refusals
protected me, a particolored
screen that makes, ironically, white noise.
I knew these other lungs
abetted me in the crime of breathing

where I could be sucked whole
into the spongy tissue, surrounded
by world, yet still alone. I didn't want
the womb which is a blank screen; I wanted
this endlessness, someone else's air pinned to
my own breath.

I wanted, endlessly. And here image
after image obliged me with
a pictorial sequence that leads not to sense
but words:

a mute, endless gorgeousness that neither eye
nor ear nor puzzled lung can translate.

Zack Rogow

Rant of a Drag Queen

NOW WHO PUT THINGS TOGETHER TO FALL
    APART LIKE THIS
HONEY YOU KNOW IT'S DANGEROUS TO LOOK
    AT THE OCEAN
I JUST WISH THEY'D CLEAN UP THAT HUGE MESS
OR ELSE TAKE ME TO THE NINETEENTH
    CENTURY
IN AN ART NOUVEAU ROCKET SHIP
SO I CAN LICK CHOCOLATE SAUCE
OFF THE BARE SHOULDERS OF MONSIEUR
    ARTHUR RIMBAUD
WHILE THE FIRST RAYS OF SUN SHAKE PARIS
    LIKE A BEEHIVE
OTHERWISE
I'M AFRAID I'M JUST GONNA HAVE TO PUNCH
    MY FIST
THROUGH THE CUTESY DRYWALLS
OF A MIDWESTERN SHOPPING MALL
I BOUGHT THIS PYRAMID OF PERFUME
CALLED ETERNITY
GIRL I'M ASKING YOU WHY
DO AVALANCHES KEEP DICING THE ANDES
AND THANK THE LORD I'M NOT THAT PERSON
    WITH MY NAME
WHO SEARCHES THE FACE OF A COMPUTER
    SCREEN ALL DAY LONG
WITH MY EYES SLOWLY BOILING

LIKE SOME MALTESE PASTA SAUCE
I'M THE LAST BLUE BLOOD
LEFT IN THIS SAD EXCUSE OF A HONKYTONK
    TOWN
OUT OF SOME LOST FILM NOIR
DID YOU KNOW I'M ACTUALLY A MEROVINGIAN
    PRINCESS
WITH A NEW FACE PEEL
THAT'S WHY I SIP LOTUS FLOWER TEA ON THIS
    BALCONY
WHILE FURIOUSLY COMPOSING NOTES
TO MY BROKER AND CONFIDANT
WHICH I'M PLANNING TO EMAIL DIRECTLY TO
    MONACO DON'T RUSH ME
JUST AS SOON AS THE TIDE BURROWS IN
FROM THAT MINERAL SEA.

Charles Cutler, Dan Mahoney & Gaby Gordon-Fox, eds.

Mark Rudman

Heteronym

1

If he uses the assumed name he can also be intimate with the nym,
    n-nymph,
who wispily inhabits Lisbon harbor and has chosen to see
    him above
    all other men in Lisbon,

none of whom   see   that she   exists.

They see her and turn away, and hope nobody saw the shift in
    expression
when they glimpsed, and turned away, from just another front

for waves fog and wind like an apparition

come alive when a wave rises, ultramarine, blurred—
as litter and detritus-infested: those shell bits that once contained
    a   creature's body …

makes the dive, to go under when it crests, below and below,
    remaining down

because time above water and time below water are not one or
the same, and it's barely completed its parabola when it runs
    toward shore

splits up, hits this artificial barrier and other idle monoliths,

and the fishermen tie their boats onto their rings
Like a hitching post. The three heteronyms and their
    perpetrator endure a certain

loneliness, isolation, or ... but since just shy of their creator's
    death
they found what he'd had in wait for them

a woman   uncannily   congenial   running a
    gamut of body types

but not pairing off.   But this was also part of the script
    that people
should look at the couple and think "what are they doing
    together?"

Why would an actress like Doris Mary Anne Von Kappelhoff
    want to bond, to be,

with a drip like Dr. Ricardo Reis? "He wasn't that bad. He did
    diagnose our son.
"The specialists the industry's guru seekers gushed about were
    way off the mark."

Charles Cutler, Dan Mahoney & Gaby Gordon-Fox, eds.

Kay Ryan

Shipwreck

> I was shipwrecked beneath a stormless sky
> in a sea shallow enough to stand up in.
> —Fernando Pessoa

They're laughable
when we get there—
the ultimate articulations
of despair: trapped
in a tub filling with
our own tears; strapped
to a breadstick mast
a mouse could chew
down; hopping around
the house in paper shackles
wrist and ankle. It's
always stagey. Being
lost is just one's fancy—
some cloth, some paste—
the essence of flimsy.
Therefore we
double don't know
why we don't take off
the Crusoe rags, step
off the island, bow
from the waist, accept
your kudos.

Miriam Sagan

After Pessoa

"To be a poet is not my ambition,
It's my way of being alone"—
Secluded among a multiplicity of selves
Like a child who traces the vast oriental carpet
With a finger, or who runs the little car model
Along the tendrils and medallions
As if they were the streets of some unknown city

A mirror is not a window and yet it might be
A passerby in the window is a fragment
Of the rainy street—one person
Contains the bits of other selves
Like a run-down theater
In a shabby neighborhood
Performing Shakespeare, or Brecht.

Night falls with its algebra
Not just subtraction and division
But the idea that X
Signifies one thing, Y another
Looking for correspondence, still you say
"Nothing returns" in defiance of physics—
And like light, "everything is real."

Charles Cutler, Dan Mahoney & Gaby Gordon-Fox, eds.

Nicholas Samaras

The Invented Man

Perhaps, I am a self-made man who worships his creator.
Perhaps, I am this gathering of stories that wove the text of me.

Or I am everything I dreamt of becoming, one heart
beating out the rhythm of its name. Or I am only

the sum of what I settled for, the choices I fell or ascended to.
Perhaps, circumstance was my god of small creation.

What matter the details? Only the narrative of the event
and its end result counted.

For each situation, I rose to the table
and became what was called for.

I became strong when strength was needed.
I grew tender when my child was born.

I assumed my occupation when I had to work.
I became my job when living rent was due.

Can't you say the same? I invented
myself as the world called me to be, caught

between the country of my birth
and the country of my belonging.

I am a fiction, the only
way I could get to the truth.

Charles Cutler, Dan Mahoney & Gaby Gordon-Fox, eds.

Ada Jill Schneider

A Thought for Pessoa
Fernando Pessoa 1888–1935

Shall I take you or leave you?
Proclaim you or let you hide
behind the cross of the Jews?
I claim you, Fernando Antonio Nogueira Pessoa,
for the list of God's chosen people.

Who can blame you, self-estranged,
prolific master of pseudonyms,
for not flaunting your Jewish past?
You, who thought about thinking
about thought, what do you make
of my proposition? Are you lighting up
another cigarette at your window?
Can you decipher intrigue in the smoke?
Tell me what your heart is thinking.
Are you willing to check out one more guise,
that Jewish mask in your locked drawer
labelled "Inquisition"?
An old family matter, shrouded in silence,
Sancho Pessoa de Cunha, condemned in 1706.
Cristãos novos on your father's side.
Jewish bloodlines, flowing in veins of secrecy,
navigated centuries of Portuguese history
through tributaries of deceit.
It floods the borders of my mind

and drains my heart,
as if someone has taken what was once mine.

Charles Cutler, Dan Mahoney & Gaby Gordon-Fox, eds.

J. D. Scrimgeour

The Sack

That town down the road, Reality,
has some lovely fountains, but
the streets are too broad,
and no one sits on the stoops.

I met Pessoa there, though,
behind the mill turned condos,
and after we'd stretched gum
over the security camera,

he gave me a sack full of sentences,
slithery and dreamlike.
I brought them to my mouth,
and my mouth thanked me,

and then caught the bus
that had stopped across the street,
the bright blue bus that seemed
like a chunk of the sky,

save for the lettering, seemingly
in dried mud across the side:
ESCARGOT.
It is not as hard as you might think

to live without a mouth, but you
must leave Reality—the gangs

of investment counselors who cabal
in some restroom you've never found

will slice your throat and make
a necklace of whatever teeth
your mouth left behind when it set out
on its glorious journey.

Charles Cutler, Dan Mahoney & Gaby Gordon-Fox, eds.

FREDERICK SEIDEL

Homage To Pessoa

I once loved,
I thought I would be loved,
But I wasn't loved,
I wasn't loved for the only reason that matters—
It was not to be.
I unbuttoned my white gloves and stripped each off.
I set aside my gold-knobbed cane.
I picked up this pen …
And thought how many other men
Had smelled the rose in the bud vase
And lifted a fountain pen,
And lifted a mountain …
And put the shotgun in their mouth,
And noticed that their hunting dog was pointing.

Lisbon

Quite frankly, *nothing much happens.*
You walk downhill all day
From the fascistically monumental Four Seasons Ritz Hotel.
I have to say,
I've had a pleasant stay.
My Junior Suite makes me feel like Mussolini, it is huge.
I think of the edifice as Salazar in stone.
Salazar's slogan for Portugal was 'Proudly Alone',
My kind of dictator.
He wanted a grand hotel in Lisbon
And arranged to have one.
I consider that admirable.
It's all downhill
From the hotel.
You walk downhill all day
On the Avenida da Liberdade and never lose your way.
You end up at the harbor. Obrigado.

And it's off in a cab to Brasileira, the café in Chiado
Where Fernando Pessoa spent so much time writing his
      immortal
Multiple-personality-disorder poems,
Now called Dissociated Identity Disorder.
That's where you find the statue.
That's where you pay homage.
He sits at a little bronze table outdoors
At the edge of the busy café tables, having an espresso

Made of bronze.
There is a chair next to his as part of the statue
So you can be photographed sitting next to him by someone.
I weep when we meet.
We bow deeply to each other.
His eyes mist over.
It is fate.
Tomorrow is Election Day 2008.
I'll fly non-stop Lisboa to Obama.

Really, the worst were the Portuguese.
But does it really make sense to talk about better and worse?
    Please!
In 16th-century Portugal, there were thirty-two thousand
    African slaves.
They came overseas in waves.
They sailed over in their graves.
It comes over me in waves.
They died and went on living. At Cabo de São Vicente, the
    black Atlantic
Spanks the gruesome cliff at the outer edge of Europe and
    gets sick,
Throwing up white.
The white is made of night.
The wrath fucks froth against the cliff.
Waterboarding makes the cliff stiff.
I voted for Obama and I ask Obama if.
Yes we can. I ask Pessoa.
I ask Lisboa. Did they know about the Shoah?

In the Footsteps of a Shadow

Yes we can.
We can do anything known to man.

It's heaven up there above the sky.
It's heaven down here, too.
I got to heaven without having to die.
It was a near-death experience with Bush 43. Phew.
But meanwhile the economy. So what are we going to do?
We're going to get through.
It's heaven up there above the sky.
Hey, it's heaven down here, too.
I love the future I won't live to see. I don't know why.
And don't even know if it's true.
Maybe I've already lived to see the future.
My multiple personalities climb to altitude on a single pair of
    wings.
Luxury Man rises to the top and Evening Man brings
To the podium the first African-American president to sing
    fado,
Chicago fado dado didi dado. Obrigado.
Please fasten your seatbelts for takeoff, we're beginning our
    descent.

That isn't what I meant.
That long-ago Inauguration Day, 1960,
In a bitter cold Washington, D.C.,
The slender prince spoke without a hat or coat, elegance,
    eloquence.
His death in Dallas practically the next day was intense.

That's how the poem began.
It's time to leave the poem behind.
People saw a god trying to be a man.
People want to be blinded, to be blind.
The tragedy of Kennedy
Decanted me.
Beautiful things that go fast have enchanted me,
But it's time to leave Jack Kennedy and my motorcycles
    behind.
It is time to attend a new Inauguration.
It's checkout time at the Ritz in Lisbon.
The bill will be considerable.
I drank tons of their best port in my Baby Mussolini Suite.
I'm inside a seatbelt on a plane. It's time to vote for victory
    over defeat.

Sieg Heil!
I said that to make you smile.
But you're not smiling.
(Why aren't you smiling?)
I said that to put you to sleep,
But you're Sieg Heiling.
I want to put you to sleep.
I think I'm falling asleep and I have a dream.
And everyone, come on everyone,
Come gather at the Lincoln Memorial!
Come together now! All together now!
And there is a woman singing.
I've fallen asleep in front of the set

And the vote keeps coming in
And millions of people are on the Mall.
And it is bitter cold.
And hopes are soaring! In the bitter cold they're ecstatically
 ignoring!

I face a yawning lion shaving in my mirror in the morning,
 roaring,
And there's my grandchild standing in the doorway, adoring—
Many teeth to brush, a beard to shave!
OK, it's not solace, but it's not nothing, still to be able to roar,
 to rave
With vim and vigour about the loss of vim and vigour.
It's sort of like a finger on a trigger
Is facing me in the morning mirror, and starts to snigger.
It's sort of like walking downhill in Lisbon
On the Avenida da Liberdade all day, but then I start to run
To get to the economy and Obama and the election—
Though I'd have to say,
I had a pleasant stay.
The breadlines in America will eventually go away,
And we will live to see another day.
A great leader lasts longer than a day.
The rain comes. The sun shines. He does not melt away.
A black man on a white horse shall chase the redskins away.

It's the dignity at Appomattox of Robert E. Lee
Live from Phoenix on TV.
That old white warrior John McCain gracefully concedes.

Nobly gives the nation what it needs.
A thousand years from now, you know it,
This day will be remembered, poet.
By the shores of Gitche Gumee,
By the shining Big-Sea-Water,
Told his message to the people,
Told the purport of his mission.
Car horns are celebrating up and down Broadway.
Tractor-trailer air horns joyously blasting.
Harlem to Times Square—Tribeca to Mecca.
Fado dado didi dado.
A nation conceived in liberty conceives.

Kids high-fiving, others crying.
Fado dado didi dado.

RON SLATE

Shame
after Pessoa

I miss things that meant nothing to me
and so much was nothing.
The world begins returning
like a sailor climbing the hill
to his house, lugging a duffle
bulging with what really happened.

As if the leaves aren't falling
in your mind. As if your memories
aren't like bright leaves falling,
so that the sidewalks are there
only because they are remembered
under the leaves, and things not remembered
are reshaped and unsaved.

I labor to defend myself
against the tedium of the telephone
and its cries of uncaring delight.

These dreams, these visions,
what a vulgar way to be released.
But the squeak of my office chair
is no better, the static of admonition
on the public address system.

My co-worker says, The nice thing
about all this is you can't miss
what you can't remember.
Suppose you had Alzheimer's.
You'd stare at the phone
and it would mean less than nothing.

Shame of the insensate rushed hour.
Immobilized in spurts on the way home,
I miss my knitted sweater,
I miss my grandmother.
Then I climb the hill
with leaves layering the driveway
and the structure of maples candidly clear.

Ken Springtail

A Paean for Pessoa

Is it over yet, Fernando?
Your statue shrugs still waiting at your / table on the square
If it's you that waits, Fernando,
And not another effigy of absence you declare
As the pigeons gravely bob
And the first few lamps / of evening griffins throb.

Nothing ever ends, Fernando,
Though attention flags and humans have to / give it up for
      lost
You were not afraid, Fernando,
Yourself to scatter like the crumbs / the lazy tourists tossed
This is not a night of masks
But a day of tanks and buzzards circling / slowly down to
      roost

There was something in the stars you saw
You could not draw, Fernando:
Crazy patterns to the way we turn
Your eyes discern, Fernando
Even as you float away
And try to say
If I had a name and origin
I'd render them, Fernando

Now the Internet, Fernando,
Has come along to rescue us / who never could before

Leave our words like you, Fernando,
Bronzed a thousand ways and read / like driftwood on the
 shore
I can hear your voice in each
Perverse soliloquy / and parody of speech.
There was something in the stars you saw
You could not draw, Fernando:
Crazy patterns to the way we turn
Your eyes discern, Fernando
Even as you float away
And try to say
If I had a name and origin
I'd render them, Fernando;
But I have no name or origin
To render now, Fernando.

David Starkey

Everything Is Absurd

> *I'm riding a tram and, as is my habit, slowly absorbing every detail of the people around me.*
> —The Book of Disquietude [163]

You stare at the dark green thread
Embroidering the neck of the pale green dress

Worn by the dark-skinned woman
Standing next to you at rush hour

You imagine the entire political economy
It took to make such a sinuous stitch

Suddenly you are jostled and rub against her
She turns to look at you

Her face is prettier than you'd anticipated
Her eyes less empty

The green thread does not mean
What you wanted it to mean

Your whole philosophy evaporates
Sweatshops and workers disappear

Yet when you return home to write
The episode down in your book

Charles Cutler, Dan Mahoney & Gaby Gordon-Fox, eds.

Like a sleepwalker you only include
That part of the dream that fixes you

Firmly in the center
You omit the part about being wrong

The Windmill

> *The path up the hill leads to the windmill, but the effort expended in climbing it leads nowhere.*
> —The Book of Disquietude [439]

Sweating in the cold, damp
skin chilled as you climb
the hill. Pewter sky
blanketing what's left
of this autumn afternoon.

The path to the windmill
wends past three boulders,
a mason's cottage, and a horse
pasture. Going down is not
the same as going up.

Of the two things Fate
has given you, the gift
of dreaming is more useless.
Beware: reverie leads
to writing books and poetry.

Your account books, though—
hoard them. Record each debit
and credit as it occurs. Soon, someone
will come calling for the ledger.
Make sure it is in order.

Charles Cutler, Dan Mahoney & Gaby Gordon-Fox, eds.

S Stephanie

Oblique Question
after Pessoa, for Bill Kemmett

In the mind there is the ball
of childhood being tossed
against a great white wall.

In the ear there is music, the jumps
and thumps and echoes of a dog
pitting itself against the enormous silence.

In the eye, only a baton,
a figure in black, his head of white
flowing hair riding above a crowd of others.

But in the blue horse of the chest, what?
That is the question,
those are the answers.

D. L. Stein

Smoke

after "The Tobacco Shop," by Pessoa as Álvaro de Campos

I'm too many others.
Sometimes I wish I could be the first one,
The one who smoked leaning against the library wall
Then sat at the café table with espresso and a book.
When I was the man who smoked, there was at least the time
It took for the brown threads of tobacco to burn
Which gave me moments of unhinged thought, moments to
        reflect.
Now, if I were to smoke, the nurse would shrug
"What do you expect? You smoked," and she'd wheel
Me out with tubes taped to my nose, the tank
Perched behind like a prison guard.

I miss the pauses during day and night
Smoking gave. After I made my daughter
I lay staring at the ceiling's punched tin squares painted white
And sank into thoughts of the future as I exhaled
How this child would unite her mother and me
A bridge between us, a passage to the future,
Spirals of smoke like wraiths, like river mist.
Her mother went to sleep without asking
The results of contemplation—I was only smoking.

Now that I've stopped smoking,
I've no time for the reverie
That sweet rough air in my nose, throat, and lungs

Provided. The other me(s) elbow
Their ways to my brain. When I look at my round-faced daughter
Putting her doll to bed, I see a young woman
And me the young man who will rake his claws
Along her back and shove himself into the very center
Of who she was. She will want that reality and think him strong,
Someone who will buy her pearls, who will protect her
From the thugs who travel in packs and enjoy taking turns.

Now that I've stopped smoking, I worry
I will not live to stand in the doorway,
My daughter's washed hair smelling of lemons
As she stands behind me waiting for the boy
To take her to a school dance I know is an excuse
For their explorations of new territory, their unmarked bodies.

Now that I've stopped smoking, I see Fate
As my older sister with scissors. Sure, I'd like to leave
For the coast, somewhere warmer with palms clicking
And oleanders growing up to the windows,
Bougainvillea twining the porch railings, mambo
And tango music from the cantina. Would I be
A different me? And what country is now free
Of officials in league with thieves, bribe-takers, murderers?

Best to stay here, make believe I know all the different
Selves who argue the existence of God, that I'm convinced
Pluto is still a planet, that this one is the only world,
And it was me, for a time, who walked beneath the blue robes

Of the Virgin, lit candles, and paused at the martyred Christ.
True, I stopped when my daughter was born; I must have thought
I would be her savior, that she wouldn't know
I was only a man who went out for a walk at night
And returned smelling of mint so he could bear
The truth that if he was created in the image of God,
Someone is laughing, someone enjoys the joke.

And tomorrow, the dog who came up and sniffed at my shoes,
And me who's writing this, get up. I put on my shoes,
Keep this barking and sniffing to myself
As I kiss my wife good-morning,
My daughter good-bye as she straps on her school satchel.
This me goes out into the street the same as yesterday
With the stones, the café, the barber shop, the canal.
They are what they are. I will turn a corner, pull a cigarette
From its flat colored box, light it, and inhale
While I wait to die. One day my daughter will tell
Her child, "There was a man who was many men,
One who believed he was my father, who existed
Only because he saw my hand, the crib, a child
Who called him 'father' and heard her mother singing."

Charles Cutler, Dan Mahoney & Gaby Gordon-Fox, eds.

GERALD STERN

This Was a Wonderful Night

This was a wonderful night. I heard the Brahms
piano quintet, I read a poem by Schiller,
I read a story, I listened to "Gloomy Sunday."
No one called me, I studied the birthday poem
of Álvaro de Campos. I thought, if there was time,
I'd think of my garden—all that lettuce, wasted,
all those huge tomatoes lying on the ground
rotting, and I'd think of the sticks I put there,
waving goodbye, those bearded sticks. De Campos,
he was the one who suffered most, his birthday
was like a knife to him; he sat in a chair
remembering his aunts; he thought of the flowers
and cakes, he thought of the sideboard crowded with gifts.
I look at the photo of Billie Holiday;
I turn the light bulb on and off. I envy
those poets who loved their childhood, those who remember
the extra places laid out, the china and glasses.
They want to devour the past, they revel in pity,
they live like burnt-out matches, memory ruins them;
again and again they go back to the first place.

De Campos and I are sitting on a bench
in some American city. He hardly knows
how much I love this country. I have two things
to tell him about my childhood, one is the ice
on top of the milk, one is the sign in the window—
three things—the smell of coal. There is some snow

left on the street, the wind is blowing. He trembles
and touches the buttons on his vest. His house
is gone, his aunts are dead, the tears run down
our cheeks and chins, we are like babies, crying.
"Leave thinking to the head," he says. I sob,
"I don't have birthdays any more," I say,
"I just go on," although I hardly feel
the sadness, there is such joy in being there
on that small bench, watching the sycamores,
looking for birds in the snow, listening for boots,
staring at the begonias, getting up
and down to rub the leaves and touch the buds—
endless pleasure, talking about New York,
comparing pain, writing the names down
of all the cities south of Lisbon, singing one
or two songs—a hundred years for him,
a little less for me, going east and west
in the new country, my heart forever pounding.

Charles Cutler, Dan Mahoney & Gaby Gordon-Fox, eds.

John Tagliabue

Weigh it in your hands, don't be noisy

Fernando Pessoa,
I weigh your name in my hand,
I feel it is like the body of a small bird,
    I hear
        its heart beat, I see the sky desiring its song,
            flight,
I figure Whitman is hiding behind a tree
            admiring,
      I will tell only a few at a time to
  notice,
we don't want to disturb the privacy
         intimacy
         authenticity preparedness
              from
          which poetry comes.

My being a poet isn't ambition, It's my way of being alone.
—Fernando Pessoa

This separation is strange, accompanies us,
I am part of my mother and yet separate from her
    and she separate
from her parents, and yet she is intimate with them though
    they are far in
the past and across the Atlantic; if the heart beats it
    has something to
do with them; and they too were initiated by others that
    are far from them;
I breathe in the atmosphere, I breathe out; we are
    part of each other
yet there is also a feeling of separation; it is the
    same with dreams
and thoughts. Can we get our Act together, we and God?
    You hear
something that was, is, part of you; breathing you
    want to
seek to understand it. You are sad when you sense
    it is
momentary. But often my being a poet is also my
    way of
        being with what I see or imagine.

Charles Cutler, Dan Mahoney & Gaby Gordon-Fox, eds.

TRYFON TOLIDES

November and Almost

Again my dreams are close but I forget them again and walk off
into the day. Parts of them hang from me
on invisible spider threads gently swinging. I get in the car and
       drive
through lit streets with poor people and box houses. Red
hibiscus. Light brown dirt. Barbeque cookers made from barrels.
Icons of sustenance.
Sunlight, pressed down onto the world. The light and all its pain
will save me.

A Vast Journey

> Every time I go somewhere, it's a vast journey.
> —Fernando Pessoa, *The Book of Disquiet*

And so that trip from the cupboard to the stove
took me to the unlived lives of dictators
shucking oysters in a vat of blood and ice.
And who walked beside me
from the cupboard to the stove
and found himself
wedged in a savannah?
And who was it finally who set the table
and could not stop adding
another plate, another glass,
while the ocean filled the pitcher,
and the clouds filled the ocean—
and my own hand—
how many lives had my right hand lived
while my left hand lagged
like a sad and awkward apprentice
setting a spoon against a napkin
as if putting the wind in place?

Charles Cutler, Dan Mahoney & Gaby Gordon-Fox, eds.

Katherine Vaz

My Prayer For Astonishment

How startling, the first time I saw a photo of Fernando Pessoa! I thought a snapshot had tumbled from my brain onto the page. My father's face is an exact match with the poet's.

The fair-olive skin and dark hair, the eyes and nose—uncanny.

The mustache and glasses—perfect replication.

Even the perpetual hat and tie—that too. My father would put on a suit and fedora to take his paychecks to the bank. His mother liked to say, "Only the rich have the arrogance to look as if they're poor."

My father and his family, and Pessoa's mother, Maria Madalena Xavier Pinheiro Nogueira, are from the same island of Terceira in the Azores, so the twinning of images could be the result of being cut from a similar swatch—tiny, sea-saturated—of the genetic fabric.

But there is an intersection of their spirits as well. The novelist Eça de Queiroz described the Lusitanian temperament as one of "jittery melancholia," and neither my father nor Pessoa could entirely avoid pressing their souls to the mold of it. I'm no stranger to it either. Out of this acuity of nerves comes self-effacement but also a longing for grandeur. There's no contradiction in that; (Octavio Paz called Pessoa "the author of paradoxes clear as water"). If someone flails like a live wire seeking a current, he'll gaze into what he thinks is a void only to find that total darkness refuses to exist; he ends up conducting stars.

Pessoa's cure was art, which he defined in *The Book of Disquiet* as "the illusion of liberation from the sordid business of being." My father taught high school in California for decades, but he painted in his every free hour, magnificently, constantly—a seascape like crushed cat's-eye marbles hung over our sofa, and when he was 19, he rendered his vision of the Last Judgment, complete with a weird tin man, on his father's car tarp—and the writerly instinct that saturated my bloodstream as a child came from witnessing such a steady answer to existence. It becomes a victory no one can take away if there's no asking for reward.

It wasn't until college, when I discovered Pessoa, that the poet fit a transparent screen of himself with further precision over my father as he sat painting. Pessoa describes (also in *The Book of Disquiet*) laboring in a "pokey office" with "grimy windows" overlooking a "joyless street." Consolation came only when it occurred to him while peering outward "... that I have as brothers the creators of the consciousness of the world ... Shakespeare ... Milton ... Dante ..." My father was a beloved teacher, never a doleful cog-in-the-machine, and he added uplift by keeping a bust of Dante near the window where he painted. Bookcases with literary works—and cookbooks and histories—lined the wall behind him.

Does one seek nothing as a means of daring greatly? Why should solitude offer such grand communions? It was Pessoa (and Kafka, and Dickinson, and Emerson, and Simone Weil, and Eudora Welty with her line about "all serious daring starts from within," and Bruno Schulz's comment about dreams exerting "an I.O.U. on reality") who taught me that every act of attention in art, even if it collapses, is a decision to realign the universe. When I copied out Pessoa's quote about shutting himself up "in the house of his spirit" in order to "further the cause of humanity," it was in part to inspire myself but also because it shocked me. It sounded like terrible hubris. But then I found I wrote best when my ego seemed lost, when I wasn't proud at all, but when I did in fact marvel how a person alone in a room can speak with the living and the dead.

As a young writer, I bought *Always Astonished*, translated by Edwin Honig, at City Lights Bookstore in San Francisco, and I came across Pessoa's prose piece, "I'm riding in an electric trolley car." The passenger notes the embroidery on the collar of a woman's dress, and his senses enter the silk thread and journey back to the factory, accounting books, and the politics of work, and they proceed further, into the dressmakers themselves. The thread of the collar tows him into their domestic realms. He goes on to "… divine the loves, the soul secrets of all those who work so that this woman before me in the electric trolley might wear around her mortal neck the sinuous banality of a swatch of dark green silk on less-dark green material." Stupefied, reeling from distant regions multiplying themselves, he leaves the trolley "… somnambulant. I have lived an entire life."

It is my most referenced excerpt when I consider how to write, when I talk to students who think that writing is about what they know or can summon as analysis. I tell them—as I tell myself—that to be Always Astonished trumps being wise. Follow the thread until you feel stupid, helpless, and weak. Writers should be jaw-dropped and corporeally defeated. (Two Portuguese verbs meaning "to astonish" are espantar, which can imply being frightened, and assombrar, related to assombração, or ghost.) In my first novel, *Saudade*, I gave what I called river-vision to my character Conceição. Her eyesight enters people just as Pessoa's had funneled into that thread, and she can remain inside them even when they step out of view.

That imaginative passageway, the thread toward deeper astonishment, relies heavily upon sensation, which Pessoa termed "the only reality in life," an antidote to the "doom of thinking." As a writing teacher, I often encounter stories ruled by the head, with judgments offered by characters who are mostly binoculars and minds. I've become alert to catching this in my own drafts. No matter how experienced a writer becomes, she must recognize a fear of taking that exhausting plunge through the electrifying green thread.

Pessoa's theory of *Sensationismo* counsels that life is best divined where sensation and silence (attention or emptiness) combust. He wrote carefully parsed sedate poems but also Technicolor bellowing ones like Whitman infused with panic. In one style, he presents thoughtfulness as if to display where we can't help but be doomed; in another authorial persona, such as in the "Maritime Ode" with its large-lettered roaring about the high seas, his poetry froths with neural firing.

Enter my father once again. A peculiar aspect of his avocation is that he ranges among wildly different styles, as if separate creators are taking turns through him. Tiny Pollack canvases, Rembrandt-toned portraits, one Matisse-like arrangement of green shades coalescing into a still life of pears. Why should any artist think of himself as a single entity with only one voice or tone?

Pessoa, in his invention of heteronyms—those light-beings he unfettered from himself with their independent histories and radically different poetry—answers the call to multiplicity in a way that's famously his own. Many writers take a scalpel to solitude, and ideas and things rise out of the slashes; with Pessoa, living people emerge, not smoky but hard-outlined. On the cover of his Latin schoolbook as a boy in Durban, South Africa, he scrawled "pessoa"—his name is Portuguese for "person"—in eerily different scripts that defy analysis. He gave his three main heteronyms—Alberto Caeiro, Ricardo Reis, and Álvaro de Campos—their own horoscopes, physiognomies, and career paths, and they in turn produced their odes, arguments, or wheeling free-verses, happy to contradict one another, with Pessoa taking dictation. Bernardo Soares is his

English-speaking heteronym, and there are fainter ones too, such as Coelho Pacheco, who has no recorded life and wrote only one long poem, dedicated to Alberto Caeiro.

It's easy to conceive of characters as the mouthpieces by which we can funnel our contradictions. Most of us get as far as fancying ourselves multi-faceted. But what if we house separate creatures that lift in and out of our trappings of skin? And isn't that what any author attempts to let loose—not imaginings, but discrete, breathing people of dimension and vast difference?

In testimony to how alive they are, these heteronyms have walked straight into the books of other authors: Ricardo Reis takes us into the fascist regime depicted in José Saramago's *A Year in the Death of Ricardo Reis*, and Pessoa himself is pursued in António Tabucchi's *Requiem*. (A student reported that the recipe for a Janelas Verdes cocktail in *Requiem* released his own skull-banging heteronyms, all of them various shades of green.) Tabucchi also composed a breathtaking elegy to Pessoa in his *Os Últimos Três Dias de Fernando Pessoa* (Quetzal Editores, Lisboa, 1997), when the chief heteronyms come one by one to bid him farewell as he dies alone in the Hospital de S. Luís dos Franceses in 1935. It is impossible to read Pessoa's gentle goodbye to his Master, the consumptive Alberto Caeiro, without being close to tears.

Here, too, I finally understood why this non-metaphysical, plain-spoken shepherd was Pessoa's self-anointed Master, rather than the tall, monocle-wearing sensationist, Álvaro de Campos, who wrote the poetry most often associated with Pessoa. Caeiro, not a hale outdoorsman but pale and delicate, was the most averse to thinking. The meaning of a fruit is to eat it; his pure inspiration is to see things as they are, to argue that art is too much of a consolation, a disguise. Caeiro would approve of Wallace Stevens'"Study of Two Pears," in which we're reminded that pears are only themselves, not viols or bodies.

When I wrote my first novel, *Saudade*, about the Luso-Americans I'd grown up among in northern California, I let my character Viriato open a Fernando Pessoa Heteronym Business so that the Portuguese who saw family members and friends dying or leaving could call upon the poet to inspire creatures dreamt in repletion. For a heartbroken man, Viriato conjured a starfish to help him regenerate, plus an 18-year-old chef, Xica (named after my grandmother). I had her scribble down some rhyming "Rhapsodies to Fat" while I watched the Super Bowl alone in my apartment in Irvine, California, back in 1991. Wall-splashing ping of unction extreme / Ooze of sardine, halibut, bream ... On it went for three stanzas. I don't remember the game very well.

There's a shadowy side to this heteronym business that's worth remembering, lest we make it too aesthetically stylish. Pessoa himself declared that the uncoiling of the poets inside him was "... at bottom an aspect of hysteria that exists in me." In men, he asserted, hysteria is manifest as poetry and silence. The grandeur of creation exacts its due, its carving of the flesh. Art may be in the name of elevation or transfiguration, but at base there's a horror of that green thread shooting out through sensation and getting knotted in the ether of disquiet, unease, illness, death. In *Fernando Pessoa Na Intimidade* (compiled by Isabel Murteira França, Publicações Dom Quixote, Lisboa, 1987), I came across an unnerving photo of the poet that activated this warning for me. He's nineteen, and his face is obscured by a white smudge on the print. Included among the six female relatives around him is his paternal grandmother, Dionísia, whom he feared he'd follow one day into the asylum. Despite everyone being crowded together, no one is looking at anyone else. The photo stuns with its almost deliberate reminder of the imprisonment of the self that no amount of stoicism or ratiocination—or art—can fully assuage.

One of Pessoa's timeless caveats—a refreshing rejoinder to these times of success-driven attitudes—is his insistence upon that unbridgeable gap. Art cannot conquer our inability to break out of our skin, our sensibilities. It was not a heteronym but Fernando Pessoa himself who directly stated the certainty of failure in one of his most scrutinized poems, "Autopsicografia": "The poet is a faker. He / Fakes it so completely, / He even fakes he's suffering / The pain he's really feeling." (The translation is by Edwin Honig in *Selected Poems by Fernando Pessoa*, Swallow Press, Chicago, 1971.)

This is in the same school as Magritte's painting of a pipe that's labeled "This is not a pipe" because it is color and a canvas, not the solace of tobacco and smoke. A poem may be racked in pain that was truly felt, written while the poet was in agony—but a poem is not that agony, it's a mask over it or a reshaping of it—no, not even that; it consists of words. Even an empathetic reader cannot grasp the pain or person whole.

And what if he could? How would that stop the failure? How would that allow us to face one another? What would facing one another alleviate?

This might be Pessoa's most helpful and brutally honest assistance to us. His resignation has the odd effect of offering to save our sanity by promising there's no escaping inexactness and separateness. And yet—one keeps on, writes anyway. It's even nobler to fight back when there's no hope of winning. In that same Pessoa-signed cycle of poems, he declared that at birth, "They shut me up / Inside myself …," and his defiant cry is, "Ah, but I ran away." If the drive toward art is based upon illusion, it is also our only recourse. Through inquiry and creation, we can at least pretend we've made shape or sense or a communion that refigures our fates. And this brand of utterly truthful pretending leads us to the highest sense-making open to us, and perhaps to that exalted consciousness that consoled even Pessoa as he daydreamed at his clerk's desk about Shakespeare or talked about furthering "the cause of humanity." The Portuguese verb *pretender* means "to claim" (think of "the pretender to the throne"), and so by pretending we exert our only possible fleeting claim.

Some friends in Lisbon told me—this story could be apocryphal, but Pessoa might enjoy a legend as beautiful as any truth—that the poets of Portugal agreed to honor him as Master with a year of non-work after he died. Imagine the cheating here in the United States of America, the manuscripts secreted in desks, the refusal to dedicate such a long phase of non-achievement! As a further tribute, Pessoa was, before the days of the European Union, on the 100-*escudo* note, sketched in blues, fountain pen in hand, a bright orange rose on the bill's reverse. And he used to lie in the Cemetério dos Prazeres; how majestic of Lisbon to have a Cemetery named "Pleasures." But a number of years ago, his body was translated to the Mosteiro dos Jerónimos. ("Translation" is the glorious definition when the remains of a saint are relocated, much as a translated poem can be regarded as repositioned on the earth.) This Monastery is where Vasco da Gama and the Virgil-status epic poet, Luís Vaz de Camões, lie in ornate sarcophagi.

But Pessoa lies apart from them, inside the cloister, below a contemporary obelisk, tucked into a corner to honor his lifelong shyness. I sometimes visit the Café Brasileira in the Chiado district, a place Pessoa haunted and now occupies as a bronze statue, but it is at the obelisk—one must know it is there, one must ask for directions the first time—that I stand with the most reverence. In this monumental spot, he is selected as immortal and yet holds fast to aloneness.

There's another gift that my own Pessoa-heteronym, my father, gave that allowed me to tunnel still farther into the poet's words: the lilting blessing of the Portuguese language itself. Readers and speakers of Spanish will also recognize, as I learned from my father, that the name "Steven" allows for wordplay and nuance that cannot be conveyed in English without a footnote. "Esteves," or Steven, practically replicates the past tense of the verb *estar*, "to be." *Esteve* means *he, she,* or *it was*. A name can add an overlay of the past, a shadow of reverberating meaning.

Here, then, is my giving back a tribute to my fellow writers and fellow lovers of books who may not know this, in the hope that it will enlarge the love for Pessoa's famous poem, "The Tobacconist," by the heteronym Álvaro de Campos.

We begin the poem with the powers of the grammatically correct double-negative to insinuate unease and contradiction. The poem's first line is striking, bare-boned: *Não sou nada:* I am nothing. At the same time, it means: I am *not* nothing. The narrator gazes out the window of his room at the mysterious, clanging, busy world and is transfixed by its contoured reality, but he senses it could be a dream. No matter; he's failed thoroughly, and it's impossible to believe in himself. He is nothing, and he is also not-nothing. He remains the man standing at a doorless wall, expecting a door to open.

In his imagination, he instructs a little girl to eat her chocolates; that pleasure is certainly worth more than his leaden pondering.

The owner of the tobacco shop visible across the street stands at his portal, and the narrator muses that both of them will die one day … and the store's signboard and this poem being written will go on to vanish.

The poet-narrator lights a cigarette. (My father was a lifelong pipe smoker; I can smell and see the white plumes.) The poet considers the lines he'll need to write (my father smoked while puzzling over what colors to choose at his easel) but the smoking liberates him from the terrors of thinking.

Electing to go on smoking as long as destiny permits, the poet lazily sinks into the idea that if he married his washwoman's daughter, he might be happy. This is so unlikely that it's stated parenthetically. Love is a whim about someone distant and removed, barely known or knowable. But even a foggy notion of a future happiness propels him to the window, where he recognizes *Esteves sem metafísica*, the "non-metaphysical Steven," so-called because all he wants is to buy tobacco in the shop.

The poem now sparks alive, jolts us; it's *como por um instinto divino*—as if by divine instinct—that Steven turns, sees the poet, and waves. The poet cries back a greeting, and the universe completely reorganizes itself for him, though without idealization or hope. The owner of the tobacco shop smiles.

Just as we should grin: If we read Steven as the past tense of "to be," then we are invited to recognize that the poet is waving at himself. If he's smoking right then, he also once visited that shop (or another one; it's the act more than the location that matters) in order to obtain his cigarettes. In the pure, Caeiro-esque act of acquiring tobacco not for any lofty reason but simply because he'd like to have a smoke, Steven—or the poet when he was the buyer in his recent past—captures a rare, perfect moment. As a dreamer-pragmatist, he's enjoying the illusion that time can achieve this infinitesimal, sensationist freeze with future, present, and past aligned. (We were informed that the poet's smoke drifts like a "personal highway," like a road ahead of him.) Eternity is amusing itself with bigger things—the destruction of all reality. The poet will still insist upon pretending that time can be seized whole, arrested. That insistence prompts the universe, out of respect and astonishment, to reorganize itself.

Not that there's hope. Not that there's no hope. The smartest option is to go on amusedly smoking, you who are waving at you whom you were, you waving at whom you are not. The poet is Steven, but Steven is separate, too—only himself.

On my desk as I write this is a miniature cartoon I cut out of the *New Yorker*—a tome labeled "Pessoa." Bookmarks stick out of the fat volume at ragged angles. Surely it would amuse him to see his name on something with the heft of a Bible.

I wrote a first draft of this essay quite some time ago, when I lived alone in Cambridge, far from my native California, on the third floor of a brick building. I got up to look out the window when I finished typing about getting up to go look out a window. The trees were shedding the last of their persimmon-colored leaves. Snow was in the forecast. The moon was riding high and hidden behind the fullness of white, a snow-pregnancy saturating the black sky.

A neighbor from the ground floor was out in the yard with her dog, Oscar. I used to run into them when Oscar was a puppy, and suddenly he was large. While it was too great a stretch to imagine them as Esteves with his tobacco, I had the impulse to wave as a sort of fun, private sense of symmetry in writing about Pessoa while acknowledging someone out of the near past.

My window, though, had been stuck since I moved in. I couldn't lift it. Because the galaxy will hardly reorganize itself or bestow alignments upon demand. Even if it was night and I was alone and it would have cheered me if life would please imitate art. My neighbor never looked up. It was cold out there. She and Oscar hurried inside.

I am reading my essay years later in New York City, where I live now, where I am happily married. The consolation is to wave at this past person I was, so serious and hopeful about art. My father passed away a few years ago. And yet his parallel to Pessoa still lives with me, and I am taken aback, in a good way, at the younger woman who took such consolation in the power of a Portuguese poet who felt enough like family to open her vision, to come calling again.

Charles Cutler, Dan Mahoney & Gaby Gordon-Fox, eds.

Marc Vincenz

When Uncle Fernando Conjures Up a Dead-Bird Theory of Everything

Chapter One

*In Which Our Dead Bird
Speaks of Epic Change in a Foreign Tongue*

(i)

In your own myopic view you exist
only as part of your own narrative,
nonplussed by mass & those bundles
of positive energy. Deep in gin, you ask:

Are there really universal truths

when particles become fields & fields, not
underlining, but dragonflying on top of a deadpan description:
symbols based on the metaphor of a bird that dies
in the natural philosophy of its own groundbreaking design?

& with the ice clinking, unpeeling

the layers of this reality shows how restless
you are, even at this hour. For no matter how
silent or how softly something deadly moves,
even a bird squashed on a little-known path to Eden,

is anything truly at rest? & yes,

light is bending toward
all that gravity converging on something
resembling to a straight line. In this billionth
of a second are we just leaves floating

upon an endless Orinoco, Ganges or Amazon?

On the other hand, who cares what occurs
four billion years from now. What is it then

about immortality—that bizarre notion of newness,
the sharp pinch of loose fingers on loose skin

when there really are no words on this page.

(ii)

& isn't every word mired in what already occurred. Being
is purely a trick of light caught in a blurring
of the here & that visual cortex weaving
in & out of the sky meeting a sea;

& upon its surface two bolts of lightning hurtling.

& didn't we arrive here in a cloud
of toxic gas amidst a whorl of radiation
our collective histories converging
upon something only visible in its own becoming?

Charles Cutler, Dan Mahoney & Gaby Gordon-Fox, eds.

You ponder the meaning of all that infinitude.

I have been told the best thing to do
is to stare into the smallest distance, deep
into a zero volume—
for there is no such thing as needed,

even in the excesses of a wild imagination.

Several times you've mentioned
your immutable sense of loss
watching those ancient footprints lead away
& how you feel somehow everything

needs to be made up.

Chapter Two

*In Which Our Dead Bird
Makes a Wretched Discovery*

All those weddings held, trumpeting up
speculation on growth & inflation, &
those Saturnalian rings within rings—

A dance of atoms, Sibyl sighs, considering

being or becoming. (*Or, more likely
the fallacy of crooks.*) *Hand me a smattering
of elixir to cleanse my soul,* she cries.

We negotiate the hours, the fire of expedience,
devouring ourselves in the bones of our knowledge,
both repelled & impelled by that agent
of immeasurable change, the coherence
of figurines that appear to mean something else.

Sibyl quotes Newton: *When bodies
            turn to light, light turns into bodies.*

Perhaps this is the most ancient memory
of the first forces of the sun's transmutation,
of the catastrophic ascent

Charles Cutler, Dan Mahoney & Gaby Gordon-Fox, eds.

of tribes
of nations
of empires
of civilizations ...

Chapter Three

In Which Our Dead Bird
Notices an Erroneous Light Rising

In the biopic of the now
(which doesn't truly exist
as we've previously established, yes?)
what is water & what is light?—

both neither particle nor wave?

by like forces that agent
an immeasurable change,
the coherence of the figures that appear—
it's all about context you've said.

Nothing remains what it is

for very long, & yet, is not
our own quantum state subtle,
negligible, bacterial—spectral
fingerprints in a haze of dualities,

the perfection of the integration

down into the heat where imperfection
unfolds into its potential—Ah!

The entanglement.
Is this where we finally wake up?

. . . .

flashes & dots & pings & ticks &
dots & lines & circles & waves & ...
no, not yet—*if the moon is there
why are we not compelled to look back?*

We are existence after all, are we not?

Ah, to fall in love with that act
of observation (whether it was
actually there)—no, not in the polarized
light hanging over the city. Yes—,

we *are* entangled you & I—

what one does the other sees,
what one sees the other does,
the other sees what one does,
the other does what one sees—

Chapter Four

In Which Our Dead Bird
Seems to Come to a Foregone Conclusion

Out in the confines of time, space
or anything else, just try to find me ...

but what when we (are) no longer matter?
moving into the shadows of the impossible?

Does the participator create the new world?

In the words of the oracle, freeing up a multi-
verse of parallel (even conjoined) outcomes,

splitting history like cells in their probable variables.
What are we aware of then, my sibylline love?

Are we nothing more than weavers or craftsmen?

fine-tuners of simple patterns?—&, the question,
can our patterns be arranged in sensible ideas?

Who has the tools to tell the whole suburban story?
Please elucidate: What do you think then is this primal urge?

Not to forage or hunt, but to know the unknowable?

Charles Cutler, Dan Mahoney & Gaby Gordon-Fox, eds.

Chapter Five

In Which Our Dead Bird
Realizes that Religion is a Form of Cryptology

A botox paradox, & once again,
looking for a missive or message
in the plurality of motions, in the shifting skies
in the stratosphere of oceans—

even in skintone & the amniotic shift

of textile on firm skin, to simplify
the ordering of sensory experiences—
order needs to emerge even when
it emerges somewhere else.

Reality must exist, surely, even

if nature itself depends on its perceptions.
So tell me now, as you empty
your last glass, tell me
of that great all-encompassing metaphor.

What disquietude we possess as we dive

into the unknown on a hero's journey
in our limitless desire to become something

of everything, not just a dot or a wave
watching constellations rise &

spin on in unspeakable desires—

is this the true measure of bliss?
beast nudging beast?
Let me hand you these fragments
of a bygone era that they may deliver you safely

into the bruised heart of a promised land.

Charles Cutler, Dan Mahoney & Gaby Gordon-Fox, eds.

Rosanna Warren

From the Notebooks of Anne Verveine

III.

I kissed a flame, what did I expect.

Those days, you painted in fire. Tangerine, gold:
one would have had to be a pilgrim to walk
through that wall of molten glass.

And purification
could be conceived, if not
attained, only after many years,

in autumn, in a fire greater than yours,
though menstrual blood still tinged the threshold
and our ex-votos were sordid—scraps of blistered flesh

taped to kitsch prayer cards—and neither of us knew
the object of this exercise, except
having, inadvertently, each of us, burned

we recognized the smell
of wood smoke, the slow swirl
flakes of wood ash make in heavy air;

and we were ready, each in a private way, to make
the gifts the season required.
Mine was the scene

of my young self in your arms,
eyes in your eyes, clutched in the effort
to give each other away—when I glimpsed

behind your pleasure, fear; behind
fear, anger; and knew
in a bolt some gifts

conceal a greater gift.
I have kept it. Now I am ready to give it back
into darker flame

in this season of goldenrod, the ardent weed,
and Queen Anne's lace in its mantilla of ash.
And yet, how lumpishly, how stupidly I stand.

How much that is human will never burn.

V.
The carpet is not a story. It is a place,
garden of crisscrossed pathways, labyrinth,
fountain, pool, and stream.

As though the fabric had ripped at the vanishing point
at the top of the street
of ashen façades and slate-sloped roofs, you stepped

through the gap, out of your own world.
I had already lost my world.
We met in a torn design

which we tore further, pulling the tall warp,
thread wrapped tightly around our fingers until it bit the flesh
and the rue de Lille unravelled.

I know about design: it's my job,
arranging other people's letters in star charts
that phosphoresce in the dark between the closed covers of books.

You knew about design from the holes
blown through your country.
We spoke in a language of no country on earth.

You moved slowly, in shadow, teaching the shadows
to echo my name. You ripped my shirt at the neck.
Was it The Beloved I held, holding you?

Down the middle of the carpet the river
weaves a thousand gray glimmers into the deeper green.
The river knows about mourning; that's its job.

How many years has it practiced? With such fleet fingers. A man
woke me at dawn this morning, sobbing and cursing in the street,
reeling from sidewalk to gutter and back again.

On my long gray street, the rue de Lille, where I still live.

VI.

You are dead, therefore I write to you.
I am dead, therefore I write to you.
Did we ever kiss? The shadow airplane

swooped down to smack the tarmac silently.
That crash didn't crash. The kiss
did but dissipated

in air like phantom smoke
rising from my shadow chimney inching
its way all afternoon across

the neighbors' slanted roof—
heat gusts escaping up the flue and printing themselves
as visible ghosts trailing

off to a chilly Empyrean.
February gleams on the roof slates.
As if the fire were real. As if

the heart pumped real blood.

VII.

Distance was the house in which I welcomed you.
But it was in the river
that we became cadence, there were the current braided

together again, after the stone bridge stanchion parted the
    stream.
It was to last only as long as the beauty lasted.
Do you believe in the soul?

Words torn from the void, wet and mewling.
Where we walked on the mountain, water
poured around us, surged up from springs, seethed

down in rivulets, rocky streams, and one long blinding cascade:
your kisses were an eau-de-vie and as bitter.
I am poured out like water.

Distance is feminine in French.
I held a knife to a man's throat and let him bleed quietly into
    a cup.
What does "us" mean?

Coiled serpentine headdress of Leonardo's woman:
you wanted her. I wanted you.
Chill sunlight flexing itself on the city river

gave me the emptiness I needed
to write these instructions: Sorrow
is a liqueur. Drink deep. We will all be consumed.

Naomi Washer

between me and the streets, and the home upstairs a fiction

Turn the camera on the rain in the street, rain in the alley. A film in black & white where someone's whispered words appear on screen: *Autumn helped us make this a reality.*

Our first film adaptation of Our Good Old Days.

We should try to take a photo. Let's enter the drawing room of this very fine house, though we never did decide about the portraits on the wall. There I am: I look like I'm posing with my hand stretching out into the world. This persona is a visually stunning experience between moods.

Like the night I watched the moon rise: I thought it was a ship coming toward me on the lake, while out in space an astronaut watched 2,000 sunsets every 92 minutes.

Let's face it: if I were okay, what would I be doing out here on this night walk with my hands? Avoiding the crowded basement of myself?

Let's take a photo. Let's zoom the camera in on all these normal people in the street. We'll rehearse our character work: *Hello! I'm a very fine house, and you look as jazz-fusion as the size of the world.* We look like when we laugh with no wisdom in our mouths. We look like people trying to find a little beauty every day, trying to find a normal day in North America. I'm always surprised by all the blending. How we lived in motion. Why do all these hours pass so quickly?

On second thought, I'm not sure I knew you. Let's take a photo to be sure. Knowing me, I won't come back for years. Keep your midnight river walks: I'll be all silver-haired and distinguished on the opposite coast. Something tells me I will not have survived my own apartment. But today is the true embodiment of my surroundings: I'm performing in the mountains, beyond time.

The way I weave my personal experience: this persona is a longstanding tradition in my room.

On screen, those whispered words appear again: *Dear So and So, I'm sorry I couldn't be here, surprised by all my former selves.* Another quiet voice responds: *Dear So and So, I'm encased in amber. Is that my hand in the sky? Do you know all those things I still don't know?*

The director would like to hear those words from your monologue again. Go ahead:

Hello! I'm a Renaissance woman—half a cherry pie and I'm to life!

But I'm suddenly conflicted. Words were calling, and satellites.

The director motioned us forward and told us to *speak, look out the window, keep moving into the room,* but no one noticed: I was happening on my front stoop, too busy with my world.

In the Footsteps of a Shadow

Remember when you said: *I'm off to the Midwest carrying essays in my bed.* You kept announcing your farewell to the stars, the tall grass and the dirty glass in all its silence. You promised you'd make a film adaptation of all this consciousness. You promised I could be a truck parked out front in the actor's dream. You promised you could conjure Fernando Pessoa in the rain, though you'd never seen those quiet cobblestone streets heading back into the night.

I may have lost today's wise words from walking through all the rooms of this year. But here's a new author photo, courtesy of me, in which I go before you—walking backwards—looking—

Charles Cutler, Dan Mahoney & Gaby Gordon-Fox, eds.

Ellen Doré Watson

In Which I Address Fernando Pessoa

Your disquiet disquiets   who *says*
    live   to think?   whose name
means person,   only feigned
    nada   achieved indelible
    dismays me———who doesn't need
dismay?   gray suit
    Emperor's   —no,
    exact   inside the suit
that suits you   get behind
    naked   draw the line
at *Understanding   wearies us*
        love   you're ripping
            my busy mouth.   Senhor,
a question: *today*   *as lucid as if*
you didn't exist,   Dear Person
            dearly dour supposed   Soares,
did you   crack a smile?   feeling
    opposed to   thinking   *a certain*
content   like that of *the mystics,*
        Whoever you are (all   ),
you are darkly   I *grasp   we are*
what we are,   beg   take back *All*   ever
been done   ridden with errors, (though yes, we
worship the *perfection*   we can't have   ). Dear
    Factless   Approximation,   approach, knowing
these hours.   like *rose petals   separately float.*

[Erasure of an earlier draft of this poem; italicized text taken from FP's *The Book of Disquiet*]

Jackie White

Voice Lessons: Fernando, To Fernando

Tell me the heteronym of your worst self, and
I'll let you decipher my handwritten diary.

Today, one of you said, I like life much less,
but we know that's a lie—it's the self that

the I loathes, and it's all over the diary—
scraps gathered from the floor of a tattered

but respectable tavern, homely and adjacent
to the depot—the self that never dared

to get on the train, so long-scrutinized, schedules
so long-studied, as if you were genuine

about going, someday, somewhere to be new.
How unremarkable, the failure to change

the face you look out of, the fixed
faces of others, the longing in your stare

as you recognize in them everything
futile, tremulously banal—the inertia

and exhaustion of wanting nowhere to go.
You return to your rented room, window

Charles Cutler, Dan Mahoney & Gaby Gordon-Fox, eds.

eyeing the tracks for you, and write more
of nothing—white confetti later to litter

the platform under strangers' feet, to stick
to their suitcases, travel ready. The head of one

self spins toward the disquieting grunt of a train
departing, which the other pretends to have boarded.

John Sibley Williams

Only Half-Blind ... and Beautiful

> *No, it isn't weariness ...*
> *It's the fact I exist*
> —Fernando Pessoa

The world vibrates
with so much energy,
dizzying us to the once lucid
unabridged and naked truth
that the miracle is simply to exist.

But just following the footsteps
we've arraigned into a life
can break apart our wheezing certainty
like warm glaciers,
boil our muscles and bones
like acid in the eyes
or a stew too small to feed
the whole family.

So often imprisoned behind tall
city walls makes us smaller
and sensitive to what we think
matters. But nothing
matters save our breath
and what we see.

I despair
only in what I miss
so I despair often.
But then I taste the world
with my fingers and nose and eyes
and am glad at least
in what is briefly mine.

My words are these taste buds
and they are not always strong.
With so much flavor, so many colors
and overwhelming feasts of sensations
oozing from the earth's every pore,
I feel unable to be one
with it all.

The weariness of consciousness.
The suffering of thought.
The solitude of understanding.
The loss inherent in wisdom.

Only when mindless
or when writing myself
out of wisdom
can I smack my lips on Autumn
and see that it will snow
by the end of this poem.
Even if I never wrote it.

Language

There is no understanding this tree
but by naming it *tree*
and affording it the luxuries
of *ancient,* lofty, rough-skinned
and *crusted by the orangest leaves.*
But stripped of all we've added to Nature,
we're want to know form.

Since sapling, it has but grown
toward the sun, not like a man grows
but wholly as a tree, avoiding the personalities
we've imposed to make it more
like man or god. As we find the nearby river
babbles and runs and glistens by moonlight
with all the lights of heaven, so too our *tree*
genuflects to wind and courageously faces timelessness
and knows all the visitors resting in its branches.
Such is the painless path toward ignorance.

Does the tree really know anything
but that it is? Each time
I blink, it sheds another description
like useless skin from long-gone snake
until it is no longer
even tall, until the birds and squirrels
scurrying within such dense foliage
are but the embraces of feet,

the pinpricks of beaks, until
finally I am nothing
except when I finger its bark. Then
I am a squirrel, a robin, the wind,
and this tree neither laughs nor sighs.

May I forever try to write like the tree
so each word weighs not in fantastical colors,
forced meaning, hurried wisdom,
but finds the page alone
in the lightness of its touch.

For Fernando Pessoa

Waking to a thunder clap that never rains,
the fat day painted white with outlines of blue
and sparkling like a severed power line
dancing in the street,
is to be born over and again,
each new sun, songbird tear, wind's breath
and bathroom mirror reflection
the first of its kind
the world has known.

As the world doesn't know you apart
from its dense garden,
what's a petunia to a lily?,
you cannot find yourself apart from it.
Mounds of shaving cream
the clouds razors zigzag down from
like the zipper that opens each question
into the simple joy of need-
less answers.

For all we need is to see
everything between exposed horizons
and walk without thought through the vast
rows of blood colored flowers and waste
not a moment on the unchangeable, to change
only pillowcases between each new life,

Charles Cutler, Dan Mahoney & Gaby Gordon-Fox, eds.

each a little larger than the entire universe.

Mark Yakich

The Teller Is the Only Survivor of the Fairytale Ending

On the eve of never departing at least there are no bags
to pack or last breaths to send away
with the last storybook lover. How lyrical it is

to be off to nowhere. No sore heart
nor new fist, no new heart nor sore fist,
no one soaring or sore at all.

But if I hear a pair of voices
coming between noises coming
from the guest room, it must be bedtime again:

I chase a couple one way across the ditch,
over a hill, through the neighbor's orchard and field,
I chase them back toward home,

corner the two against a fence.
Then after a lot of praying, I pull the keys
from the dead man's pocket while cupping her

breath in my hands. It sounds like a foolish thing
to do: to stop a couple of heartthrobs
between If and Then.

But telling is a terrifying
beauty, who gives and gives and gives out
prematurely. All the sadness in life

lies in the present moment.
It's not that the characters truly remember being
born, but that's The Story.

I, The Teller, promise them the future
lasts a long time. And then I head into the unending
rain with a borrowed umbrella,

one I have no intention of ever giving back.

You Are Not a Statue

And I am not a pedestal.

We are not a handful of harmless
scratches on pale pink canvas.
Today is not the day to stop

looking for the woman
to save you. What was once
ivory is wood. What was once

whalebone is cotton.
My coif and corset are duly
fastened, and your shirttail is

tied in a diamond knot.
You may be the giver
of unappreciated nicknames

and the devoted artist
who has given my still life
life. But we can never reach

each other's standards.
You want to condemn me
to eternity. I want to make you

Charles Cutler, Dan Mahoney & Gaby Gordon-Fox, eds.

no more perfect than you
used to be. We are not
together, we are not alone.

Nocturne

If time is the sky,
Then moments are understandable

Autumns, the leaves split
Seconds, and sorrow is
Undressing the neighbor boy

In a single breath.
If such gusty emotion is

The landscape, words make
Only the mountains, and the valleys
Are just gorgeous inversions.

And if the head sounds
Like that, each drop of rain

An amorous dialogue,
Then leave tonight,
Between the wave and the lantern,

Every particle
Rowing.

Charles Cutler, Dan Mahoney & Gaby Gordon-Fox, eds.

Yours and Some of Mine

To be wanted before you're wanted, painting
flesh in a badly lit room. To run away,
figure slapped over ground,

quickly and clumsily, then perfectly
smoothed in, as if by small rhapsodic blows
to the sternum. To take those short

precluded trips to the minimal
hotel in town, to the lobby, to that chair
from which I, Infinite Reader, watch

a man's hand slightly touch the blue-
belted hip of his lover. I heard you
clear your throat periodically. The hours

I was obliged to watch, with lips pulled away,
a supernumerary copy of your figure
reappearing as ground, vanishing

into what was never really there.

Brenda Yates

Excerpt: A Review of *Absolutely, Positively 4th Street*

... as for the title poem it too keeps to itself. In fact nothing is known of "I" at the outset (perhaps expected by now of this author) . Strangely, nothing is revealed in its course, an oddity offset only by a growing sense of narrator presence. What are we to make of fragmented references to Pessoa, Dylan, Rushdie, Wallace Stevens, Borges, Unamuno, T. S. Eliot and the *Oxford English Dictionary?* But let's begin with the title. Call up a famous song by arguably one of the 20th century's greatest songwriters, and already a reader is alert or perhaps even slightly hostile; imitation so often breeds weakness.

The second notable choice is no better—an epigraph from Fernando Pessoa: "Am I thinking about everything, / Or has everything forgotten me?" It is worth noting that Pessoa wrote a lot about identity and in fact created several. None were mere pseudonyms inasmuch as they wrote in different styles, critiqued or reviewed one another's work, and had entirely separate biographies.

When venturing into Pessoa territory, witticisms spring to mind, such as: "The self-division of the I is a common phenomenon in cases of masturbation." Or "the more I worked on *The Book of Disquiet*, the more unfinished it became." Or that language was a scalpel to cut to the heart of truth, which he did not believe in, and to the heart of himself, which he also did not believe in. He did, however, consider himself animated by various ideas not the subject of this review.

Yates seems haunted by a concern that one's angst may be sophomorically self-indulgent. (Don't forget Dylan's classic line "you got no faith to lose and you know it.") The speaker, like Pessoa, has "lost all respect for the past," and aspires to "factless autobiography"—demonstrated by a self-aware beginning that exists only to set up the recursive mechanisms in play throughout. First, the strategy steeps the body of the poem in religious allusion. "Faith," "God," "anoint," join images of shroud, rain, roses, fisherman-like spiders, a heavenward-leaping worm, as language slips back to its sacred-seeming origins. Speaking in meditative fragments, the "I" moves through its cruxes in the form of an inclusive, indirect discourse, an effect used to draw the reader in.

We become "I" knowing, for instance, that faith, a gift, can never be an act of will, that some of the most powerful tragedies in western literature concern its loss. We get inklings of Eliot's "Ash Wednesday," of Unamuno's *San Manuel Bueno: Martir*, of Stevens' "Sunday Morning," of the Borges character drawn into an encyclopedia entry about another world, as well as his book review of a tome that never existed (which now we want to read).

We know belief is not unwavering, that even saints struggle with doubt. But worse is Unamuno's parish priest who continues to nurture, to save others though he, himself, is beyond salvation because he has lost his faith. We are kin to him, to that writer—who sought truth in life and life in truth, even knowing he would never find them—and to Yates' speaker, given to seeking. We understand paradox—Salman Rushdie noted there was no vocabulary to speak of the spiritual except the religious, yet religion is the poison in the blood as well as the great solace and inspiration. We know art began as sacred—and that sacred, "at its best, brings about great masterpieces, and at its worst, murders."

Though Yates has been criticized as descending into indifference, I would argue instead that in this book and its title poem, she evokes the way we know what only humans can, eyes open. This despite the fact that rain, spiders, shrubs, cats and of course, the universe, don't care about struggles to understand the world or to label its parts in order to bring ourselves some comfort.

It may be that her "I" weighs in with a Buddhist sensibility of mindfulness, or can be seen as having some spiritual relationship with nature, but even so, we aren't allowed to forget the sadness and futility that accompany consciousness. We keep in mind how frequent these thematic arcs are, as in, say, Defoe's *Journal of the Plague Year* or Camus' *The Plague*. And of course, we must consider etymologies.

There's a history of confusion between imminent and immanent—that indwelling or abiding, as of the Deity. Consider, too, the latter's secondary denotations that make the distinction of acts performed or occurring within, rather than outside the mind of the subject. Implicit is the fact that one of the earliest gods was the sun—which carries through history, as in: "May the Lord bless thee and keep thee. May the Lord make his face shine upon thee." Attending to roots in the hypothetical proto-language of origin wherein words like shine, sheen or show have connotations of behold, of radiance, of brilliance, we find they begin to define one another, adding illuminate, glisten, shimmer, luminous, glow, along with beam, ray, halo, as in the appearance of ... which are then often compounded with deity or divine.

And so a speaker weary of trying to find an expression lacking that, concludes in the only vocabulary available—a likeness to God.

Even a word such as *beautiful* can't be fully unlocked from *beatific*, and thus *to bless*, where the OED makes an aside thusly:

Charles Cutler, Dan Mahoney & Gaby Gordon-Fox, eds.

"Hence, a long and varied series of associations, heathen, Jewish, and Christian, blend in the English uses of bless and blessing."

I would argue that these are in fact blessing poems.

[From *Reviews and Essays, 2000 to 2015* by Willes Christian]

Amy Yee

Assignment #5: Pick a Word in Your Own Language and Describe What It Means

Chaam.
You'll know what it means when I tell you:
I say it when salmon is 12 dollars a pound at Stop & Shop.
Chaam. I say it when gas costs $3.20 for one gallon.
I say it when I see men on TV dressed like women
so they can win a million dollars,
when my son yells because the Red Sox lost again.

Chaam. I said it years ago when my son fell in the bathtub, when
I saw the black hole in his mouth and my daughter cried and
      splashed
in the red water. His mouth full of blood, he said:
"*I was pretending to be Godzilla.*"
Chaam. I said it when I saw blood
on my daughter's face and I hit the cat for scratching her again.

Chaam, I said when I walked past China Wok
and saw they had no customers on a Friday night.

I heard my neighbors screaming again through the walls.
Chaam. I said it quietly though I knew they couldn't hear me.

Chaam. I said it when I saw on TV tall buildings burning,
when I saw people jumping from rooftops.

Chaam. I say it when I tell my children how lucky
they are to have so much to eat, remembering
when I was their age, I took care of four of us,
even my older brother, how we all fought for two boiled eggs,
how my father hit me with a can of salted fish
when I took ten cents from his wallet to buy Vaseline.
Chaam. My lips were so dry.

I said it last night at dinner.
I eat so fast that my children
laugh. They say I "inhale." I laid
my chopsticks on my bowl, not one
grain left inside. I wiped my lips and watched them laugh.
My stomach full, I sighed: *chaam.*

Contributors' Notes

Accardi, Millicent Borges
Pessoa represents the freedom to don new identities (heteronyms) and luxuriate within and inhabit language with an equal sense of both drama and humor. To shoulder the notion that identity can be a flexible construct.

Ansel, Talvikki
I'm grateful to the translators who have made it possible for me to experience Pessoa's writings. In the early 90s when I was in graduate school at Indiana University, David Wojahn introduced our poetry workshop to Pessoa's poems. I read, and reread, *The Book of Disquiet* and the poems translated by Richard Zenith, Edwin Honig, Susan M. Brown, and others; I borrowed books from the library, copied passages into notebooks and onto scrap paper, and pondered phrases I couldn't get out of my head. I was entranced by the voices, and how one writer's poems could express various ways of being, and lives inhabited. In Pessoa's poems, the narrators were distinctive and the city of Lisbon took on a magical and tangible quality—though I had not yet had a chance to visit. When I did go to Lisbon years later, it was startling and strange to actually see, in a museum, Pessoa's typewriter.

Ashton, Sally
In 2011, I was invited to teach in the Disquiet International Literary Program in Lisbon, the city where Pessoa lived, imagined, and wrote his many lives. Richard Zenith's translation of *The Book of Disquiet*, together with his essential introduction, was a required text. And there in its pages and along Lisbon's cobbled streets, I found "that episode of the imagination that we call reality," a disquieting adventure with its kaleidoscopic perspectives well-suited to both Pessoa's modernist era and my own frame of mind. How could I not have heard of him before? But then of course, "Fernando Pessoa, strictly speaking, doesn't exist." If you believe I do, find out more at **sallyashton.com**

Bakken, Christopher
My poem in this anthology starts off with "At times we wish that we could disappear," a line that begins to convey my fascination with and

admiration for Pessoa. His poetry constructs such a multiplicity of identities and voices that there is ample space to dissolve every kind of boundary: egotistical, perceptual, aesthetic, and spiritual. He was, in the Keatsian sense, a "chameleon poet," a playful ventriloquist with mystical tendencies. His poetry constructs "a negative space even knowing can't fill," as I put it in another line, and it is therefore a rich source of inspiration for those interested in beauty supported by a scaffolding of doubt.

Baller-Shepard, Sue
For ten years I worked on a project with partners in northeastern Brazil. I'd been listening to Forró music, at their suggestion, and such leanings made me curious as to what poets might have inspired them. Fernando Pessoa was not named. That not-naming interested me. Discovering Fernando Pessoa later through another Portuguese-speaking friend, I understood my Brazilian friends' hesitancy to mention him. Yes, Pessoa is Portuguese, not Brazilian, but obviously it went deeper than that. Today Pessoa is all over the map, making a ruckus as translations of his work continue to appear. According to Richard Zenith, there are close to 40 English translations of his "Autopsicografia" alone!

Pessoa resonates with me on several levels. A translation project in graduate school, for example, suggests parallels with his writing. One of my final exams was translating Psalm 24 from the Hebrew Masoretic text. How many ways could it be translated, given the Hebrew verb-subject-object word order and pronoun shifts, which biblical Hebrew affords? How many ways could those words be rearranged to make meaning, given the text? Pessoa's work comes to mind. Always, whose voice is it: his, one of heteronyms, a semi-heteronym like Bernardo Soares? Pessoa writes, "I am merely the place / where things are thought or felt." Right, he is the vessel through which language, ideas, others flow. We get to reap what he's sown, what came through him, "To the I I know: I write."

Always I love to read an original thinker, hear an original voice and Pessoa has some seventy-one of them. His verses are "like jewels, / Able to endure into the far future."

Barnstone, Aliki
For me the tug of Pessoa spans the years. Edwin Honig, my beloved professor and friend at Brown University, translated Pessoa. I am a

translator myself, and so early on I inhabited other writers' identities. Like so many Greek Americans, I am obsessed with history, especially erased histories. Reading Pessoa wasn't only an example of the way one could write persona poems in a technical way but in a spiritual way— and I found myself channeling my imaginary poet, Eva Victoria Perera and transcribing her lines as her voice spoke to me or within me, and I found myself there with her in Thessaloniki, escaping Thessaloniki, and pretending to be a Christian on Easter. Even now writing those words, I feel her sorrow and panic for her daughter and her capacity in the face of horror to see with a heart of beauty and love.

Bassis, Aileen
Pessoa (as evidenced by this anthology) was a fascinating figure in his embrace of other personalities and voices. In our current time of writers frequently being defined by their identity, it's particularly liberating to think of a writer with a panoply of selves. My poem was inspired by poems written as Alberto Caeiro, "the keeper of sheep" who thinks with his eyes and ears, reveling in the otherness of the natural world.

Bernstein, Charles
Je est un Pessoa.

Biespiel, David
The entirety of my adoration for Pessoa, or Pessoas, is this: I love his unwillingness to concede anything to a reader. I love his disregard for enchantment, his barbed emotional intelligence, the manner by which he labors, the many looks and shadows, the dreams, the friends, the ghosts, the wounds. I love how his writing is, from beginning to end, a canvas of alertness to the "hidden orchestra" of the soul.

Blaustein, Noah
Decades ago, when I wrote this, I was wandering around somewhere between my penchant for narrative and lyric poems and what the latest crop of intellectual bravado was espousing: that narrative poems lacked rigor and that all poems should be kaleidoscopic. I was trying to exorcize the ghosts of graduate school. Like the sampling the DJs used to do, I began to "sample" lines from Apollinaire, Stein, and whoever. I wasn't

accountable to any thesis advisor anymore. I could follow my curiosities. With his heteronyms and other personas, Fernando Pessoa didn't contain his multitudes, he inhabited them. He presented an alternative for me. The line that generated the poem reprinted here came from "Don't Clap Your Hand Before Beauty." I was tired, at the time, of poets making everything pretty to be published. I still had a bit of the mosh pit in me. The opening quatrain grabbed me, the idea that "beauty isn't meant to be felt much" and "It's the shadow of the gods." I think I was watching new neighbors move in across the street with their dogs so, loosely channeling my inner Pessoa, I decided to write the poem from the voice of a flea, to be beauty's shadow, the itch that is felt, even in the midst of ecstasy.

Bradley, John
For me, Pessoa is both a common and proper noun that means: 1.) There is no Pessoa; there are only many (lower case) pessoas that you piece together in the hope that you might create the entity we call Pessoa. 2.) If you want to find the (lower case) pessoas you embody, you must eat a moon-boiled page of Pessoa. 3.) No, it doesn't matter if you've stroked the headache Pessoa once nailed to the ceiling. 4.) Álvaro de Campos kindly agreed to write me a series of letters, which appear in "my" book *Hotel Montparnasse: Letters to Cesar Vallejo*. Did Pessoa compose the letters written by Álvaro de Campos? Pessoa sneezes into a vase. 5.) Should you want to write a heteronym poem, you must sleep a mute sleep, inhaling a vowel once digested by Pessoa. 6.) There is only one Pessoa and his name is all the names the protozoan rain gives to Pessoa. 7.) Pessoa will be the last person, of course, to tell you that you and I are heteronyms created by Pessoa. 8.) No, it doesn't matter if you unravel the carpet and use the threads to make a replica of Pessoa's hot water bottle. 9.) In the beginning, there was only a small lump of nothing and when Pessoa spat on it he heard a voice say, *Pessoa is both a common and proper noun.*

Browne, Jenny
I bought a copy of *Poems of Fernando Pessoa* at City Lights Books on a visit to San Francisco in 2004. I had a new baby and an old job tending bar. I was also getting ready to begin graduate school at the UT's Michener Center for Writers and working on what would become my

second book of poems. It was a time that had me feeling perpetually fractured, as if performing a new role, a new face by the day, if not the hour. Into this moment, as if conjured up, Caeiro arrived, then Campos, then Reis. Let yourself break then make yourself again they seemed to say. Be plural like the universe. Words that carried me along, and carry me still.

Buckley, Christopher
What I find compelling in Pessoa is his authentic, human voice, the unflinching metaphysical doubt, the arm wrestling with God, as Pessoa appreciates the beauty and irony of the physical world where we are likely to remain no matter our hopes. From *The Keeper of Sheep*: "There's metaphysics enough in not thinking about anything."

Burton, Sue
It was many years ago. Pessoa introduced me to Álvaro de Campos—and it was love at first sight.

Carpenter, Bill
I was a Pessoa fan from my first encounter in the 1980s. I eventually used the Biblical title "A Keeper of Sheep" as the title for my own novel *A Keeper of Sheep*, published by Milkweed in the early '90s. The protagonist was a young female college student expelled for political activity who ended up as a caregiver and ultimately a euthanist for a composer dying of AIDS. "A Keeper of Sheep" seemed like the right title, and a tribute to a writer who very much influenced my own work. When the poet says, "I never kept sheep, but it's as if I'd done so," he seems to speak for all novelists who write outside the sphere of their own experience, as I did writing about euthanasia in the first person of a young woman 1/3 my age.

Christmas, Frank
More than for his sometimes maddening struggles to reconcile mind and body, thought and emotion, I read Pessoa for the way his work can look on the page. The sense that it was recklessly written, or a draft that he planned to revisit but didn't, is fair compensation for the occasional mental gymnastics he puts his readers through—as is the

overlapping world he inhabits with his heteronyms; his fondness for mock-haranguing the reader; his tirade against symbols and his litanies of likes and dislikes; his indulgence in plainspoken, non-poetic language (*just hold your horses!*); his repetitions and reversals, his repudiations of self (*I'm me, and what the hell can I do about it!*); his extensive use of dashes and ellipses, exclamation and question marks. These things—the direct, the playful and jovial—personalize the poems for me. Pessoa's suspicion of the sentimental and the feeling might seem bloodless but it's not, it's where we meet him. Now, *get those metaphysics out of here!*

Czury, Craig
I was making poetry writing happen with adults & juveniles in prisons, shelters, afterschool programs, psych hospitals, and with middle school "at risk" teens when I first read Álvaro de Campos' "Tobacco Shop" (trans. Edwin Honig). Blew my freakin' heart apart. Students, the broken students, wrote themselves inside out while listening to me read this poem as a prompt for them to write while listening. There's no deeper conversation than what gets said between a poem and its reader needing to respond with their own words. "Deep calls to deep" (Psalms 42:7). I picked up Bernardo Soares' *Book of Disquiet* (trans. Margaret Jull Costa) and was instantly transported to Pessoa's upper floor of a certain respectable tavern in its preface, where I eat in any country where I don't speak the language but have my most private and intimate conversations with my reflection in the wine glass, the window, my reflection in the silverware, in the startling street sounds and pantomimes with the saudade of my alter-ego.

Davis, Jon
I discovered Fernando Pessoa in a Portuguese Literature class at the University of Montana in 1983. I had been writing dramatic monologues and often felt swept away by the poems' speakers, feeling that I was speaking with the undercurrent of an entire life beneath me. When I read that Pessoa wrote "thirty-odd poems, one after another, in a sort of ecstasy, the nature of which I am unable to define" I recognized the feeling of my own writing as others. In my case, I was hearing the voices of people I had only a tangential connection to—a street preacher, an astronaut, a grandmother, a death-wish biker, a lonely wife. After

discovering Pessoa, I began welcoming the voices into my writing life, and, instead of writing one-off monologues, I began writing multiple poems in each heteronym's voice. Eventually I began appearing in public as one of them, Chuck Calabreze. Chuck arrived when he began writing letters critiquing my editorial stance in *Countermeasures*, the literary journal I co-edited. He later became a poet and an active heteronym, giving readings around town, visiting another professor's classroom, taking over my own classroom once a semester, and introducing visiting writers. Chuck eventually read in Kenya, Vietnam, and Cambodia. Over the years, I have written and published poetry and prose by over 15 heteronyms, most of whom remain secret even to my closest friends. My response to Pessoa has been visceral, not theoretical; he opened the door to an impulse I might have ignored.

DeCarteret, Mark
I'd go years without sleeping. Pessoa's poems on a loop. In a pool of light underwritten by the moon. Pulling my selves together. For what good it would do us. Pessoa's poems on the bed stand. Piled up to the dead stars. I'd drawn on the window shade. Lip-read once on a dare. While still at a loss. For all but a pulse. What I managed to slip out of his hand. I'd first been tipped off by Simic and Strand. From yet *Another Republic*. Pitting poet against poet. Well before I could work up a spit of my own. Pessoa's transmissions starting in mono, then stereo, before being mouthed in the thousands. Soon, resisting the idea of history altogether. Or this version of life. One's served these papers. Sparing it the land fill. Part trap door, part sunroof. I proof the tapping from under the floorboards. Read strands of light into the thunder. Nothing sitting well with us. The worlds we haven't the words. The words we haven't. Not even the pills they've enlisted. The silence that keeps. Speaking ill of us. Or the line, next to nil, I'll ex out. Take for everything it hasn't. Where I'll be telling him again. Just how tired I am. Of never getting this right.

Dolin, Sharon
What I particularly love about Pessoa (whose name, coincidentally means *person* in Portuguese) is his creation of heteronyms and his writing poems, in very varied styles, under these different heteronyms, as well as under his own name. His heteronyms, as all Pessoa readers know,

are not pseudonyms. Each of the major ones has a distinct biography and style. At the Fernando Pessoa Museum in Lisbon, I remember being struck by the desk and business cards that Pessoa had printed up for his heteronym Ricardo Reis who was deemed to be a medical doctor as well as a poet. Some writers are interested in creating worlds; Pessoa was interested in creating beings who wrote poetry. I think of him as the literary counterpart to Rabbi Judah Loew of Prague who created a golem to protect the Jews. Pessoa's heteronyms are like poetic golems that protect Pessoa from ever being fully contained in a single personality; they are his poetic efflorescence and are the expression of what I see as his Whitmanian desire to "contain multitudes."

Dryansky, Amy
I stumbled on Pessoa, an accidental and providential attraction. I think I picked up a used copy of *The Book of Disquiet* while in my grad program, struggling to churn out the required number of poems per month, hoping somehow that they were "good." Pessoa suggested a different course (or alley), where you might just trust yourself to be yourself, or more accurately, ignore yourself and get out of the way. Immersed in his work this poem came to me in one piece, and even though it was totally unlike my other poems, I trusted it immediately, I'm not sure I'll ever feel that way again. "All of this however has nothing whatever to do with any will of mine."

Dutterer, J. Paul
In the 21st century, novels are generally stale or sordid, and poems tend to be just journal entries. Either the written word has run its course, or something else is needed. A century ago, Pessoa was pointing the way to something better than traditional fiction and poetry. Because of his own high standard for himself, his works have aged better than almost any other author of his time. When I write, his example prods me to create something adventurous, artistic, and—if we can use this word in connection with Pessoa—honest.

Ehrenberg, Erica
There is a line in Pessoa's *Book of Disquiet* where he asks, "what is the space between myself and myself?" This is exactly the kind of move that

has drawn me to Pessoa over the years, not least because, for me, there is a deep humor in it, which I feel lives alongside its utter seriousness. He is both playful, and a person who has dedicated his life, as if it could not be any other way, to the exploration of his own internal states, popping out at the end of his own thoughts somewhere with a view of the universe beyond earth. It's a stance I find to be both wild and a deeply accurate way to capture what it feels like to be alive, and how little we know about what we are and where we come from. There is a hopefulness for me in Pessoa that comes from the sheer vastness of the possibility he sees inside the unknown, as if we contain within us a deep creative wisdom in spite, or perhaps because of, our fundamental lack of certainty.

Emanuel, Lynn

Through his heteronym's, Álvaro De Campos, outrageous and hilarious poem, "Time's Passage," Fernando Pessoa, a Portuguese modernist, taught me how to read Walt Whitman. Until Pessoa, I retained a straight forward, American reverence of Whitman—the democrat, the man of the people, the shape shifter. *There was a child went forth every day, / And the first object he look'd upon, that object he became,* says Whitman. To which Álvaro De Campos replies *"I...The sweaty ring on the shirt collar of the sick tutor going home."* And— *"I'm an absolute king in my feeling of kinship / … In a heartfelt embrace I hold / … the matricide, the fratricide, the incestuous, the child molester."* As a young writer, reading "Time's Passage," I was promptly educated and deliciously scandalized. My love of Whitman suddenly became very complicated. Pessoa's (Álvaro De Campos') appropriation of Whitman elucidated my American simplification of him. "Time's Passage" is a tough love poem. It celebrates Whitman with stunning astuteness, magnificent mockery, irony, hilarity, genius, and irreverence. Reading it, I was changed, and, years later, was inspired to write my own love poem.

Feinstein, Sandy

I first read Pessoa by accident. I was in a museum shop in Lisbon when I noticed a small volume of his Portuguese poems translated into English. I was familiar with the name, but not the work. After reading that book and others, I realized Pessoa was his own translator of selves and so language and translation could serve as yet other alternative identities.

Despite my Portuguese being limited to *bom dia* and *obrigada, vinho* and *mar*, limiting the possibilities of appropriation and embodiment, I could think aloud about how writing and reading as different selves could push words where they might not otherwise think to go.

Fillmore, Mary
Discovering the heteronyms of Pessoa brought me more comfortably into the variety of voices in my own poetic being, so I could write not just in different forms but from different kinds of consciousness. My longtime teacher Deena Metzger speaks of the self as a community, and Pessoa has embodied that for me on the page, allowing me to stretch the spectrum of my own perception more than I could have imagined. Because of my family's roots in the Maritime Provinces of Canada, I was brought up on photos of the foggy sea and the great ships. The romance of the sea and sailors has always called to me. My father longed to see Europe but only did so at age 50, as a university garden designer, and Portugal was the place he felt most at home. Pessoa makes a home for me, and versions of me, in poetry.

Gaspar, Frank X.
As I think back to my first encounter with Pessoa, I can vaguely triangulate the time. I had finished my first collection of poems and my first novel, both rooted in my Luso-American identity, so this would have been about the year 1999. I had been invited to read at Brown University, where I met George Monteiro and Onésimo Almeida. Onésimo, recognizing I needed more reading from the Portuguese, loaded me up with books (quite literally, armloads), one of the many generous moves from friends who opened up new worlds for me. Among the books were collections of Pessoa. I was fascinated immediately, but when I reached *The Book of Disquiet*, I was bowled over. I was reading my own mind! But please don't understand me too quickly: I don't mean I identified with his genius and nerve—I mean with the chaos and catastrophe, the vagaries and certitude of uncertainty, things I recognized in myself. But Pessoa's aesthetic solutions, his heteronyms, are eloquent, and we know them well, and in this he beggars us. He does not feed the hungry or heal the sick or clothe the naked—he gives these beings of his psyche verve, life, personality, free will. He gives or

they take; in Pessoa's inner landscape there is no difference: he begets. Without Pessoa's enormous influence I would never have recognized Renata Ferreira as my own heteronym. I would never have known to let her take me over. She would never have written her poems.

Gastiger, Joseph
I was twenty-three when I discovered Fernando Pessoa, who, if he chose, could become anyone or nobody at all. Forever, "the one who wasn't born for it ... the one with all the promise ... the one waiting for the door to open at the wall without a door." That mysterious stranger who eats his small supper alone in the same café, night after night. Mystic and clerk who did all he could to become someone who'd vanish, someone who never was.

Many poets have found we can access some forgotten longings, impressions, sensations, daydreams, when we are able to surrender to some other voice. One of mine belongs—or used to—to Cedronello Tardino. He composed "These Two Worlds" and "When All One Does Is Look" and sixty-eight other lyrics, published in his one and only collection, *Prisoners of Gravity*.

"Honey and Gall," with its balalaika, docks of Odessa, sherry and sesame, comes from a Greek-speaking émigré who fled from Trebizond in 1923.

Here is the paradox that Pessoa helped me resolve: When I write as myself, sometimes, in poetry, I find it hard to say simple things outright. I dissemble, dress myself up as someone I'm not. When I speak through a persona, I find it easier to be honest—or to be vulnerable, which is sometimes much the same thing.

Glenn, Laura
Reading certain lines of Pessoa's poetry, especially those by one of his alter egos, Álvaro de Campos, I feel like I'm in the midst of my own stream of consciousness instead of his, or that we are sharing thoughts. Some of those thoughts turn from meditative to jarring—or the reverse—seamlessly as a slipknot that can be undone by pulling a free end of the rope.

When de Campos says, "I, who often feel as real as a metaphor," he draws attention to his unreality as a character created by Pessoa, while he also speaks for Pessoa; but is de Campos (as a stand-in for Pessoa) simultaneously made hyperalive via metaphor? It's fascinating that Pessoa didn't just create characters, he brought his multiple literary personas to life through their own writings, and through them he lived on the page more than in his actual life. Pessoa primarily wrote from male vantage points, but at times he expresses a remarkable (for his time) gender fluidity of thought in his poems.

One theme that arises throughout Pessoa's works involves pain in life, as well as in art, which is something poetry contends with. Some of his poems create an uncanny sense of being immersed in emotions that he protects himself from. My poem in this anthology, "Faking It," responds to "Autopsychography," a poem by Pessoa himself, not one of his personas. "Faking It" toys with how we can make things better or worse when we express feelings through the arts.

Goldstein, David B.

I first encountered Pessoa while I was living in Portugal for the summer, and his language captured perfectly for me the coexistence between antique and modern sensibilities I found there. I recognized in this master of intricate personae the ever-shifting frames of reference I inhabited.

Gray, Robert

Fernando Pessoa found me in 1996, when I was working as a bookseller in Vermont. While shelving new books, I casually opened one by an author I'd never heard of and landed upon this sentence: "I was born in a time when the majority of young people had lost faith in God, for the same reason their elders had had it—without knowing why." On first impression, the writer seemed observant, cranky, amusing. There was something irresistible in the way subtle humor emerged from veiled sincerity. I flipped to other pages, read random passages, not yet aware this was a perfectly reasonable way to approach Richard Zenith's new translation of *The Book of Disquiet*. I bought that first copy for myself before it ever hit the bookshop's shelves, and have been Pessoa's reader ever since. "I've made myself into the character of a book, a life one reads," he wrote. I know the feeling.

Green, Timothy
I came across *The Book of Disquiet* at a used bookstore around 2003. I've always felt that poetry is both a kind of prayer and a kind of magic—and so every book of poems might as well be a bible or a spellbook. It was immediately clear, flipping through the pages, that Pessoa had crafted a set of especially powerful incantations. The prose poems (which is what I would call them) transformed and transported me and left this poem of my own as a record of wherever it was that I went.

Hales, Daniel
Pessoa levels up on Whitman's assertion that he "contains multitudes." Pessoa isn't one of my favorite writers, he's four of my favorite writers. In high school, decades before I'd even heard of Pessoa or heteronyms, I wrote poems using two different names: Phillip Grey wrote spare, moody poems and the other guy (I forget his name) wrote absurdist, satirical poems. Over time I learned to reconcile these voices, as well as welcome many new selves onto the page. Though I publish with the name on my birth certificate, the desire to evade the constraints of identity persists in another medium: I release music under four different names. I gravitate to artists who actively resist homogeneity and labels, who continually push and expand notions of self rather than comfortably consolidate them. Pessoa's project is a radical embrace of paradox, a badass act of nonconformity. It's profoundly generative at the same time that it's artistic sabotage, creative suicide. What artist wants their best work attributed to someone else? Bernardo Soares may be the Pessoa I love the most due to his haunting masterpiece: *The Book of Disquiet*. Soares' entries plumb the disturbing "endevolada" (Pessoa's neologism for dark, veiled depths), yet the book's constantly lit up with passages of stunning lyrical beauty and wisdom, like this: "I myself, am the center that exists only because the geometry of the abyss demands it."

Hardy, Myronn
It is Pessoa's ability to make new voices, new lives, innovative aesthetic choices that connect me to his poetry. His ability to fully inhabit another, imagine another, and save his lived self for his lived life is the draw, the gravity that pulls. Ultimately, it is his vast imagination I admire most, the possibilities he has unbolted.

Harlan, Megan

"Poetic license" is a term I take very much to heart when writing poems. In contrast to the other writing genre in which I work—creative nonfiction, where I can explore all the ways truth is indeed stranger than fiction—poetry for me provides endless possibilities of identity and imagination, of inhabiting voices, experiences, and perspectives that invoke subtle and crucial essences of my own life even as they sidestep literal fact. No poet has ever opened the doors onto these possibilities like Pessoa. His genius I believe is rooted in his being essentially a city poet, one offering the most generous and flexible creative scope within complex, even chaotic urban settings: to locate the human beyond the ego, through visceral details, personal qualities, and specific events that could, in a twist of fate or parallel universe, belong to any one of us. Pessoa's work taps directly into these pure veins of potential experience: the great poet of the parallel human universes all around us, ones we may inhabit through his voice.

Holland, Walter

I identified with Pessoa's poetic sense of himself as composite alter egos. I grew up in semi-rural Virginia and can identify with "Alberto Caeiro" and his childlike wonder at nature and calm innocent acceptance of the grim but beautiful reality around him. My lengthy formal education brought out "Ricardo Reis'" cerebral, detached, melancholy manner and his preoccupation with fate, mortality, the vanity of wealth and the folly and spectacle of American culture. My father was a physician, and I inherited his bedside manner and serious, sobering outlook on suffering. I've lived in New York city most of my adult life, traveled the world and often fashioned myself as a modern-day flaneur. I began to embrace "Álvaro de Campos'" motto "to feel everything in every way" and "The best way to travel is to feel." I became excited by urban life and all its many possibilities. Pessoa captured my discontinuous nature. I've played a parlor game, switching imaginative versions of myself—modern dancer, physical therapist, writer, critic, administrator, world traveler, all the while knowing underneath I'm a rather nostalgic, sadly introverted fellow who in his mind wanted to be everything at once.

Hoover, Paul
Sociolinguistics teaches that we alter our sense of self several times in a single day, depending on the company we are keeping. We are father, son, employee, lover, the person who takes out the trash, and the person speaking faulty Spanish in a call to Coyoacán. The person we call our "self" is a fluid being equipped with a language, biological and linguistic identity, and the desire to please others. This shape-shifting is subtle and also obvious. It is an act of self-translation. Pessoa formalized his multiplicity by adopting, by the count of his translator, Richard Zenith, 78 different writing identities, four of which are presented in Zenith's *Fernando Pessoa and Company*: Alberto Caeiro, The Unwitting Master; Ricardo Reis, The Sad Epicurean; Álvaro de Campos, The Jaded Sensationist; and Fernando Pessoa himself.

I was undoubtedly influenced by Pessoa in writing Sonnet 56 (*Les Figues*, 2009), which consists of 56 different formal versions of Shakespeare's sonnet 56.

Huenemann, Charlie
Pessoa serves up the haunting reminder that you are never quite who you think you are, but you aren't anything if you don't play at being someone. He is in company with Kafka and Beckett in this regard, all of them undermining selves with ruthless, surgical precision

Irwin, Jason
I began reading *The Book of Disquiet* in 2012, when my first marriage was dissolving. The more I read the more I felt like Pessoa, or his many alter-egos, were speaking to me personally. It felt as if I were the one writing the book, that in its pages I found my own life. In the end I gave up with only 30 pages left, tempted at one point to throw the book out my car window. I found *The Book of Disquiet* full of prophetic insight as well as some of the most poetic and depressing prose I'd ever read. It remains one of my favorite books, one in which I return to in snippets like *The Letters of Van Gogh*, and the New Testament.

Jemc, Jac
I heard about Pessoa for the first time as a senior undergraduate. I immediately read everything I could find—which wasn't much at the

time—and got the parentheses and ellipses that fill in the gaps of Richard Zenith's translation of *The Book of Disquiet*—(...)—tattooed on my wrist, right at the pulse point. I wrote my senior thesis on the heteronyms. I was obsessed. I still am.

Kalamaras, George

What Pessoa Means to Me, Or How I Spent My Pessoa Vacation:

I have spent many warmths / in the / in-between / many liminal / limps / the glimpse / of mouth / I say / unto thee / unto / myself / be a mask / wear a mask / be a voice / wear a voice / see the insides / of things from / the insides / where the I we thought / dissolves / into the I we are / be a mask / wear a mask / once trees along the / and the road I walked on was / a woods I drove through / the fish-shaped lantern / the ocean's / deep / metaphors mixing / the voice we thought / to give unto the world / was a voice we had not yet / become / be a mask / a voice / all the lost parts / call them / Portugal / call them Álvaro de Campos / call them what / we call calling / out to / Ricardo Reis / Alberto Caeiro / Portugal and the purposeful pupae of moths / hiding in / themselves / the summer months / all the baggages / the many warmths / of mouths / the I's / the / he's / the she's / stuffed into a single way of / speak / be a voice / wear a mask / be a mask / wear a voice

Kartsonis, Sophia

Pessoa because: So many years ago: a broken heart and broken mind. The pieces on the floor were fragments, fractures, broken things. The voices in his poems: mosaic, collage, Kintsukuroi, chorus. Why I still turn to Pessoa: because out there is too much self-certainty with too little reason. I live in the country with a good human, and lots of critters. The voices are various and true. We can only be so many selves in our short lives. We can be so many selves in our short lives. Because the late, lovely, Francois Camoin said that he was often mid-speech before realizing he utterly disagreed with himself. Because how comforting to sing against the wall of ourselves, voices splashing back against our faces, in harmony, or resounding with our own out-of-tune echoes.

Ladin, Joy
I stumbled on Pessoa in my mid-20's, after a lifetime of dissociation that made it hard to write what was then the mainstream American poem—short, sincere first-person narratives or lyrics rich in precisely observed perceptions, feelings, and images. Pessoa's example liberated me by demonstrating that dissociating from my personal "I" could open me to utterly different voices, perspectives, modes of being. I followed the example in two of my most ambitious works, *The Book of Anna*, in the heteronym of a poet who was a Holocaust survivor living in 1950s Prague (winner of last year's National Jewish Book Award) and *Shekhinah Speaks*, poems designed to give voice to the female aspect of the divine (selva oscura 2022). Pessoa enabled me to grow into myself as a poet by teaching me that I could, that I needed to, let go of the self—my individual self—as the foundation, container, and limiting principle of my poetry.

Lighthart, Annie
Annie Lighthart is an Oregon poet and teacher who, many years ago, found a freedom in the works of Fernando Pessoa that she had found nowhere else. His heteronyms opened a little door in her mind she had not seen, and when that door led to another door inside, and then yet another (each with their own style, their own remarkable weather), she began reading and writing with all doors and possibilities propped open.

Lorenz, Johnny
My first taste of Pessoa's poetry was "Autopsychography," with its famous first line: "O poeta é um fingidor." Then came *The Book of Disquiet*. Once, while visiting my father in San Francisco (my parents are Brazilian immigrants to the U.S.), in a shop of used books I happened across a bilingual edition of *The Keeper of Sheep*, a collection of poems by Pessoa translated by Edwin Honig and Susan M. Brown. In this volume, there is a poem in which the speaker imagines life as an oxcart, with only the need for wheels, traveling up and down the road until one day, at last, being discarded. I wrote a poem in which the oxcart speaks from the bottom of the ditch.

Margrave, Clint
In the 1990s, I worked at a bookstore and a co-worker handed me a copy of the New Directions abridged edition of *The Book of Disquiet*. Had I read it? No, I'd never even heard of it. Hardly anyone had in the US, at the time. It felt like a secret discovery. He was mine. All mine. From the moment I opened the book, I knew he was something special. I'd always been an outsider and reading the words of this speaker who lived an isolated life in Lisbon, similar to mine in LA, writing alone in his room, somewhat nihilistic but honest, philosophizing about existence, the self (selves), and feeling removed from the rest of humanity, I immediately connected. Within a year or two, I got my hands on a few other books, and eventually would see more translations of his work. In 2015, I finally made it to Lisbon, and to the Casa Fernando Pessoa where I got to see his typewriter and the trunk where his manuscripts had been. By then, Pessoa had become better known in the US, but I was still taken aback by what a revered figure he was in his home city, country. I guess I had grown used to poets being ignored. In Lisbon, he was everywhere. And though I was glad to see it, I must admit to feeling a tinge of nostalgia for those early days when I first discovered him, and naively thought he was all mine.

Marvin, Cate
I love all of the poets that Pessoa was mostly because he was so outrageous. He shows me (in his many versions) how to veer from standard narratives, how to loom large and shrink (I think of "Tobacco Shop")—how to be verbose, vulnerable and generous. I am a huge fan of Albero Caeiro's "The Keeper of Sheep" for his assertion: "I have no desires and no ambitions. / To be a poet is not my ambition. / It's my way of being alone." I think that one, as a writer, can learn from Pessoa much about the pleasures of employing a certain grandiosity in gesture. In short, voice. He is a genius when it comes to voice.

Mastores, Constance Rowell
Some twenty years ago, when I first encountered the work of Fernando Pessoa, I was struck in particular by the poetry of his heteronym, Alberto Caeiro. Poems such as "On an incredibly clear day" and "Not to think of anything is metaphysics enough" excited my imagination, awakened an

energy that had begun to fade away. Now here was a presence whose views on God and nature reflected my own!

Or was it, rather, that his rendering of that relationship was so beguiling, so daringly simple, so archly beautiful that it was not so much a matter of kinship—of him being like me or of me being like him—but a renewal; a re-aroused interest in a forgotten way of being, of seeing; an unexpected accord with a world in which there is no "true and real ensemble"; where "nature is parts without a whole." His poetry made me wary of unity. I needed parts. I needed pieces!

Some might find Caeiro's take on "what we see of things" to be facetious, fragmentary, anti-poetic. Perhaps. But I found it liberating: a turmoil of colors tumbling, wind flashing the privacy of an enormous escaped world.

Medeiros, John

As a homosexual writer of poetry and creative nonfiction who is of Portuguese descent, there are not many literary role models to whom I could turn to help me understand my role in the larger canon. Notwithstanding the dearth, two Portuguese poets who have helped shape and advance my artistic development are Mário de Sá-Carneiro and Fernando Pessoa. Both are intensely passionate poets who, while never openly embracing their homosexuality, have intentionally written great works of art with strong homosexual undertones.

Yet unlike Sá-Carneiro, who wrote to descend into his inner self (as many gay writers do), Pessoa was a labyrinth of over 70 writers whom he referred to as heteronyms—each with different personalities who often engaged in dialogue with each other. These alter egos were part of a larger complex being and served as a means for Pessoa to escape the inward rather than explore it—to illustrate a richer and more textured whole rather than the sum of its parts. Doing so granted Pessoa a certain freedom, and this freedom is crucial for homosexual writers of today. While it's all too tempting to typecast homosexual writers and to place our books in that small LGBTQ section in the back of the bookstore, we need others to understand our complexities and to see the variety of our galaxies that make up our larger universe. Pessoa and his heteronyms opened the door to that discovery.

Merrill, Christopher
The sheer volume of his poems, written under a seemingly infinite variety of heteronyms, is endlessly inspiring, since it suggests vast poetic worlds to be explored by his apprentices—a sacred guild which I am proud to belong to.

Moure, Eirin
For me, the tug is the humour in the insouciant sincerity of the voice P creates for Alberto Caeiro. Pessoa's relationship to language, and personal history, were compelling too: he was Portuguese but largely educated in South Africa in English, and was a commercial translator, like me. When I translated this work, in early 2000, I did it simply to let the humour emerge, realizing humour must be contemporary to be funny, or it needs footnotes. So I made the translation contemporary, is all. There was only an "international Pessoa craze" in French, not in English, in 2000. In fact, to reduce the text burden on the cover of *Sheep's Vigil by a Fervent Person* (2001), my anglo Toronto publisher removed Pessoa's name, leaving only mine! Pessoa just didn't seem important to them! Faced with my protests, a stamp was created and the rest of the title stamped inside each book. The first reprint (of many) brought the whole title back to the front cover, where it's been ever since.

Ray, Jennifer Silke
When I want to bounce out of narrow versions of reality and the world as it's usually described by objective minds, when I want to feel my full infinitude, I turn to Fernando Pessoa. As Dostoevsky and Kafka anticipated the modern, Pessoa anticipated the postmodern, as well as much that is contemporary. When he looked in the mirror, he saw his own dissolution into various identities that led to nonidentity, and he had the courage to pursue this understanding in his writings, no matter how labyrinthine and unwieldy the results. Autofiction feels very contemporary in its ubiquity, but Pessoa was certainly a godfather of the genre. We talk, today, of writers of the pluriverse like Irena Sola, whose "When I Sing, Mountains Dance" is told from the perspective of various humans, dead and alive, as well as a deer, mushrooms, the rain, and the earth, itself, and how this multivocal approach might better reflect reality as we truly experience it. Fernando Pessoa was a

forerunner of this literary movement in that he embraced all his inner selves and employed them in the form of his heteronyms to express his various perspectives on dreams and reality. He's a fitting companion to our era's infinite distractions of mind, yet also wise and so, so funny.

Robinson, Elizabeth
What compels me about Pessoa's work is the way he embodied Rimbaud's idea of the "I" as an other. I am fascinated that he developed that otherness in such depth and with such multiplicity. In responding to his work, I wanted to take on that freedom and intensity. It seems a powerful way to explore the nature of identity itself: taking on the persona(e) of a writer who was working under a variety of personae.

Rogow, Zach
Part of Pessoa's genius was that he understood, long before this became a commonly held perception, that one heteronym is not enough for a human being. And by extension, one avatar, one gender, one life is not enough for a human person, with all our facets.

Rudman, Mark
I was first made aware of Pessoa when my friend and mentor figure Mark Strand was assembling *Another Republic* with Charles Simic. They were all high on Pessoa. The translations gave me little indication that Pessoa was a great poet. In the meantime, I wrote a series of poems in an unnamed persona whose purpose was to allow me to say essentially the opposite of what I, the "real" Mark Rudman, would say in the poems I considered—is sincere the right word? My nameless persona poems were published in journals and created something of a stir. I am speaking of "Abilene," "Cheyenne," and an elegy for Cesare Pavese called "Turin: Albergo Roma," among others, in which my goal, indirectly, was to report in a deadpan fashion a series of lies, which of course had their element of truth. Robert Pinsky was surprised to hear that my reportage poems were structured around the principle of lies. Early in the 21st century, having finished *The Rider Quintet*, which was written in dialogue with a "spectral inquisitor." Someone on an awards panel referred to it as "the most complex persona in American poetry." I finally created a character in the manner of Pessoa, whose work I now

appreciated largely through the new translation by Richard Zenith and the enthusiasm of other friends who said things like "you sometimes sound" (in my real poems) like Álvaro de Campos. So I invented Sandrine Laurent, in whose voice I wrote a book, nearly all of which has appeared in journals, called *Palescon*, an imaginary Palenque, where she had gone to shoot a film in her role as mixed media artist. "Her" poems were snatched up instantly wherever I sent them and I kept going, off and on, until around 2018, since when I have tried to assemble "her" book for publication.

Sagan, Miriam

I was probably in high school when I first started reading translations of poetry from numerous languages and traditions. It helped keep me from being provincial as an "American" but what struck me the most was a kind of lucidity and emotional clarity that seemed missing from my own contemporary scene. Not confessional, and almost archaic in tone, but very open-handed towards the reader. In college, there was a fad for Cavafy and Pessoa—perhaps not a likely pair, but a sign of sophisticated taste! Pessoa of course plays a kind of hide-and-seek, well beyond that of the usual persona, but I really didn't understand that at first. I was just drawn to the poems. Of course, I find his biography fascinating—but really all poets are fascinating, whether they live in hermits' huts or inside multiple personalities. I can't count him as any kind of direct influence—that would be like being influenced by a smorgasbord. Rather, like an array of delicious things to eat, I find him nourishing.

Samaras, Nicholas

Pessoa, for me, illuminates the multiplicity of internal voices, the facets of our personalities. He reminds me that I and everyone are not merely "one thing." We are complex people who may use poetry to highlight that complexity.

Schneider, Ada Jill

Fernando Pessoa died in 1935, the same year I was born. Sixteen years later I dated my boyfriend Ron who became my husband for the next sixty-five years. When Ron died recently, my heart broke. What Pessoa said in "Birthday," I say.

"Stop it, heart! Don't think! Leave thinking to the head!... If only I'd filched the ... past and brought it away in my pocket!"

"If I Think for More than a Moment," I know "The sun may gild the face of the days, but soundless space reminds us it's just a facade: In the night all things are erased."

From Pessoa's grave in Portugal to where I stand at my husband's grave in Fall River, Massachusetts, Pessoa speaks to me "[You were] only given one vision of the things that exist on earth, and an uncertain mind and the knowledge that we die." At that, I beg my heart not to think about it.

Scrimgeour, JD

I first read Pessoa in the late 1990s, when I started to build my personal canon. I admired his audacity, how he "lived" his heteronyms through their writing, never pulling back the screen (as if there is anything behind the screen, or as if there is a screen at all). He's a poet that I return to, and I still teach him occasionally in my graduate courses, where I find myself trying to explain him: Don't expect there to be more there there than there is.

Slate, Ron

For me, the core of Pessoa radiates from *The Book of Disquiet* in which two aspects, his work and attitude, have engaged me for years. First, there is nothing self-crediting in him since he perceives humanity as fundamentally mystified and mystifying, including himself. Second, as for his self, it cannot be depended on to remain in place for analysis, and it is protean in its appearances. And yet while all of this churns and settles in his writings, he delivers to us a recognizable world, simultaneously perceived and envisioned.

Starkey, David

Those of us who write a lot, and who write in different genres, inevitably adopt different voices for different occasions. I'm drawn to the way Pessoa has amped up our natural inclination to split selves and turned that sharing out of personas into a such remarkable oeuvre.

Stephanie, S
I am drawn to Pessoa writing in different voices. Each one having its own personality and tone. I think it is such a creative way of describing all the human emotions. The many people we are inside, or could be …

Tolides, Tryfon
Not dreams or imagination (on which my poetry relies minimally), but Pessoa's acute and vivid observations of life happening just outside his window, so that he has contact with the world but at a remove. A pathological need for remove, a refusal to join in. Refusal, fear, frozenness, uncertainty. He's resigned to being a nothing, it seems. A sadness or apathetic moroseness about anything being possible, yet insisting on the song of language. Insisting, making. Insisting on making. These are some of the qualities and moods that may have drawn me to Pessoa, ones I may share with him. And our birthdays are one day apart. But I hadn't touched base with his work for a long time after drifting back to Greece, to the village and house I was born in. I've been living here for the past fifteen years or so, and not having brought any of my Pessoa with me, I had to go online for poetry and excerpts from *The Book of Disquiet* to recapture his vibe in order to write this note. It seems as if I'm still drawn to him for some of the reasons I state above, perhaps a sign that nothing has changed in my life. Confirming what Pessoa would tell me: that nothing can change because it's too painful, risky, or a waste. Except maybe for watching. But watching is also a waste although somewhat bearable if writing comes from it.

Upton, Lee
Pessoa's defiance of the conventional strictures of singular and calcifying identities and his embodying of new imaginative possibilities are lures for me. His persistence as a writer dedicated to creating multiple voices and routes for expression is inspirational—and aspirational for many of us.

Vaz, Katherine
My essay touches upon how my attachment to Pessoa began: My father bore an uncanny, startling resemblance to him. Pessoa to me was a heteronym of August Vaz, and August Vaz was a heteronym of

Fernando Pessoa. They shared Azorean heritage, wore the same glasses, liked the same hats. My father was poetic, studious, independent, and flamboyant in his way. Dad studied horoscopes, and painting was his poetry, and sometimes his moods, like Fernando's, drifted into sorrow, a lowness. Then a swerve came, into humor, uplift. Pessoa was my father's physical-spiritual twin from my start, my uncle. I've loved him from my beginning, just as I did my dad, and this has wavered not at all for either of them, not ever.

Warren, Rosanna
"I multiplied myself to feel myself," wrote Pessoa's heteronym Álvaro de Campos in "Time's Passage," elegantly translated by Richard Zenith, who had to multiply himself in order to translate Pessoa's multiplicities. But then, as Campos wrote of his creator's meeting with another heteronym, Alberto Caeiro, "Fernando Pessoa, strictly speaking, doesn't exist." What gorgeous permission Pessoa granted me, in the late 1990s, to step outside my own singular identity, my daily existence as an American bourgeoise, mother, wife, harried associate professor of literature, hurtling around the outskirts of Boston to pick up children from day care and staying up to 1 a.m. correcting student papers. As if conjured by Pessoa's wand, Anne Verveine appeared to me: an obscure poet, single, French, mourning her departed Uzbek lover, an artist who had returned to his own land. She was also conveniently dead, or at least, had disappeared, last seen hitch-hiking in Uzbekistan in 2000. Unlike Pessoa, I need only one heteronym: for a while, Anne Verveine lived my other life.

Washer, Naomi
I discovered Fernando Pessoa by accident. I came across *The Book of Disquiet* in a bookshop when I was 20, before I had published any of my own work and before I knew anything about the literary world. I was studying acting; I'd been an actor all my life. In *The Book of Disquiet*, I encountered a voice wrestling with the same questions of identity, masks, persona, and the self that I had always wrestled with as an actor and a young artist struggling to find my way. In retrospect, I can't imagine a better way to have been introduced to Fernando Pessoa, and it has been important to me to maintain that connection to his work within

a kind of privacy. More than any other author whom I read and loved as a young person before I entered the bewildering world of publishing, Pessoa remains for me an anchor; a touchstone; a reminder of why we need words to help us wrestle with our lives and the world around us.

Watson, Ellen Doré
Charles Cutler has been sending me to Pessoa for as long as I can remember—no doubt since we first met, back in the '70s after I called and prevailed upon him to tutor me from basic Spanish to Portuguese, in anticipation of a year in Brazil—and thank heavens. He's the most capacious and enthusiastic reader I know, across all genres. I worried that my lukewarm response to Pessoa's poems might dampen our friendship, but he's a bigger man than that—and *then* he turned me on to *The Book of Disquiet*, Pessoa's "Factless Autobiography," which Pessoa himself described as having "the dreaminess and logical disjointedness of intimate expression." Charles's inscription read: "For Ellen, with Ol' Fernando let us sneeze to the point of metaphysics." Amen! To this day, I can and do open that book at random and inevitably find strange and brilliant things to chew on for days, which—whether I chime with them or beg to differ—often tug me toward some unexpected new poem of my own.

White, Jackie
I was long ago attracted to the multifaceted quality of Pessoa's work—his heteronyms and their various aesthetics—having encountered his *Book of Disquiet* while building my library of contemporary Spanish and Portuguese language poets. Shortly thereafter, a friend gave me his *Selected Poems* without being aware of my newfound interest. That serendipity seemed a fitting match to the sense of jest and paradox that amused me in Pessoa's poems; to the interrogation of identity or personality that he so richly explores, as though my friend and I were one, and "each of the poems of [ours] explains it!"

Williams, John Sibley
It doesn't surprise me at all that Pessoa has grown in popularity recently. There's just something intangibly pure about his work, something inherently timeless, something both rooted in earth and

human experience and highly figurative and universal. His language is always crisp and clear, genuine and vulnerable, heavied by weightlessly beautiful phrases. He is both a poet of minutia and firmament, of humanity and ether. "To think a flower is to see and smell it" (from "The Herdsman") is such a deeply celebratory concept. In many ways, it's conceptual without the need for a concept. Like all Pessoa's work, it is so utterly simple it's shocking it hasn't been said a thousand times before. But it hasn't. It took Pessoa's unique perspective to discover something so intrinsic. Speaking of celebration, which I believe is at the heart of all his poems, there's the line "We too, of our lives, must make one day" (from "Discontinuous Poems"). To me, this summarizes Pessoa's legacy. It takes all we have, a lifetime's worth of struggle, to truly "make one day." And Pessoa never ceases to remind us, nearly 100 years after his death, to keep trying to make each day its own small, essential celebration.

Yakich, Mark

I discovered Pessoa while living in Brussels more than 25 years ago. I was just beginning to read and write poems, which was an outgrowth of my journaling. I came across Richard Zenith's translations of *The Book of Disquiet* and an originary chord was struck in me that still reverberates to this day. Later, when I began to examine and understand, to some degree, that Pessoa wasn't only putting on masks à la Pound's personae, but actually inhabiting other beings in his heteronyms, I felt an aesthetic then spiritual connection. If I ever experience a writerly low, all I have to do is go to the bookshelf and locate the dozen translations of his work where I can find a commiseration like no other.

Yates, Brenda

Pessoa continues to electrify because he is utterly original. For more than a hundred years, his poems have been as modern as that of any modernist and now prove as postmodern as any today. I feel certain that whatever future styles are called, he will be that too. It's not enough to say Pessoa writes in different voices or that he writes personae poems. He bends generally accepted ideas of poetic voice and inhabits each person created. Call his inventions multivalent, fractured or avant-garde, the truth is his multitudes cannot be contained. Anyone who discovers his work is profoundly influenced. He inspires experimentation and still feels as alive as his art.

Yee, Amy
How can people reconcile different facets of their identity, or indeed, their different identities altogether? This was something that W.E.B. Du Bois grappled with in his famous essay about "twoness". This resonated with me after I came across Fernando Pessoa and his concept of heteronyms. These were not pseudonyms or masks to hide identity. Rather, they were legitimate identities all their own. They were extrapolations, re-iterations, carve-outs or hyperbolizations of identity given free rein to grow from the smallest vestige, or to expand in ways not consciously explored.

This concept of multiplicity of identity fascinated and liberated me. I could see how disparate voices, memories and identities that were part of a person to varying degrees could be encapsulated in one. One could be immigrant, yet native born. One could carry the weight of being poor with being a world traveler. One could be Asian and post-racial. One could be withdrawn observer and lush indulger. One could be both abstract cryptic and linear realist. One could exist in the memories of a murdered child or in the world of a lover's sleepy eye. They were not just multitudes, but multiplicities.

Publication Credits

All work appearing in this volume is published with permission of the authors.

Charles Bernstein's "Autopsychographia" from *Recalculating*, University of Chicago Press, 2013. "At Pessoa's Grave" from *Topsy-Turvy*, University of Chicago Press, 2021.

John Bradley, "Footnote on a Line by Fernando Pessoa" from *You Don't Know What You Don't Know*. Copyright © 2010 by John Bradley. Reprinted with the permission of The Permissions Company, LLC on behalf of the Cleveland State University Poetry Center, www.csuohio.edu/poetrycenter/

"The Day After Tomorrow" from *The Rain In Portugal: Poems by Billy Collins*. Copyright © 2016 by Billy Collins. Used by permission of Random House, an imprint and division of Penguin Random House LLC. All rights reserved.

"Ode to Fernando Pessoa" from *Burn and Dodge* by Sharon Dolin, © 2008. Reprinted by permission of the University of Pittsburgh Press.

"At the Restaurant," from *Different Hours* by Stephen Dunn. Copyright © 2000 by Stephen Dunn. Used by permission of W. W. Norton & Company, Inc.

"Walt, I Salute You!" from *Then, Suddenly—* by Lynn Emanuel, © 1999. Reprinted by permission of the University of Pittsburgh Press.

"Salutations Fernando Pessoa" from *Cosmopolitan Greetings* by Allen Ginsberg. Copyright © 1986 by Allen Ginsberg. Used by permission of HarperCollins Publishers.

James Hannaham, "Seeing and Thinking," "Felt," "The Person in the Question," and "The Death of the Critic" from *Pilot Imposter*. Copyright © 2021 by James Hannaham. Reprinted with the permission of The

Charles Cutler, Dan Mahoney & Gaby Gordon-Fox, eds.

Permissions Company, LLC on behalf of Soft Skull Press, an imprint of Counterpoint Press, **softskull.com**.

Excerpts from *Sheep's Vigil by a Fervent Person* reproduced with permission from House of Anansi Press, Toronto. Preface, English text, and translation copyright © 2001 by Erín Moure. The Portuguese text is taken from the third volume of Fernando Pessoa's *Obras Completas: Poesias de Alberto Caeiro* (Lisbon: Edições Ática, 1979) and was originally published in 1946.

"After Pessoa" from *Map of the Lost* by Miriam Sagan. Copyright © 2008 University of New Mexico Press.

"Homage to Pessoa" from *Poems 1959–2009* by Frederick Seidel. Copyright © 2009 by Frederick Seidel. Reprinted by permission of Farrar, Straus and Giroux. All Rights Reserved.

"Lisbon" from *Nice Weather* by Frederick Seidel. Copyright © 2012 by Frederick Seidel. Reprinted by permission of Farrar, Straus and Giroux. All Rights Reserved.

"From the Notebooks of Anne Verveine, III," "From the Notebooks of Anne Verveine, V," from *Departure: Poems by Rosanna Warren*. Copyright © 2003 by Rosanna Warren. Used by permission of W. W. Norton & Company, Inc.

"From the Notebooks of Anne Verveine, VI," "From the Notebooks of Anne Verveine, VII," from *Ghost In A Red Hat: Poems by Rosanna Warren*. Copyright © 2011 by Rosanna Warren. Used by permission of W. W. Norton & Company, Inc.

www.ingramcontent.com/pod-product-compliance
Lightning Source LLC
Chambersburg PA
CBHW031312160426
43196CB00007B/503